Name _____ Date _____

Activity: Numbers 0 Through 5

 You can count to
show the number.

Count. Write the number.

1.

2.

3. Draw a set of 1 through 5 items you find at home.
   Count. Write the number.

Use with text pages 7–8.

Activity: Numbers 6 Through 10

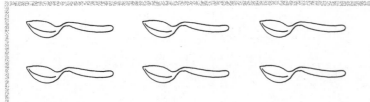

You can count to show
the number.

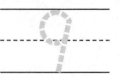

Count. Write the number.

1.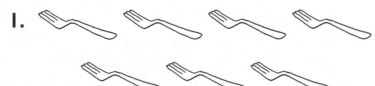

_____
- - - - - - - - - - -
_____

2.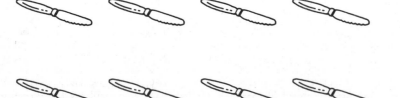

_____
- - - - - - - - - - -
_____

3. Draw a set of items you find at home.
Look for a set of 6 through 10 items.
Count. Write the number.

_____
- - - - - - - - - - -
_____

Use with text pages 9–10.

Order 0 Through 10

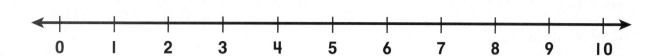

You can use a number line to order numbers.

The number just before 10 is __9__.

The number between 5 and 7 is __6__.

The number just after 6 is __7__.

Use the number line. Write the number.

Just before	Just after	Between
1. __8__, 9	6, _____	4, _____, 6
2. _____, 6	2, _____	3, _____, 5
3. _____, 4	4, _____	8, _____, 10

4. Choose three numbers from 2 through 9.

Write your numbers in the chart.

Write the numbers before and after your numbers.

The Number Before	My Number	The Number After

Use with text pages 11–12.

Name _____ Date _____

Compare 0 Through 10

You can compare numbers using the words greater than and less than.

10 is ___greater than___ 4.

6 is ___less than___ 10.

Write greater than or less than to make the sentence true.

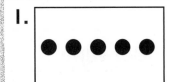

1.
5 is ___greater than___ 3.

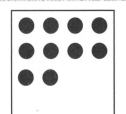

2.
8 is _____ 10.

3. 6 is _____ 9.

4. 7 is _____ 4.

5. Write any numbers from 1 through 9 under My Number in the chart.

Then fill in the other columns.

A Number Less Than	My Number	A Number Greater Than

Use with text pages 13–15.

4

Name _____ Date _____

Activity: Numbers 10 Through 15

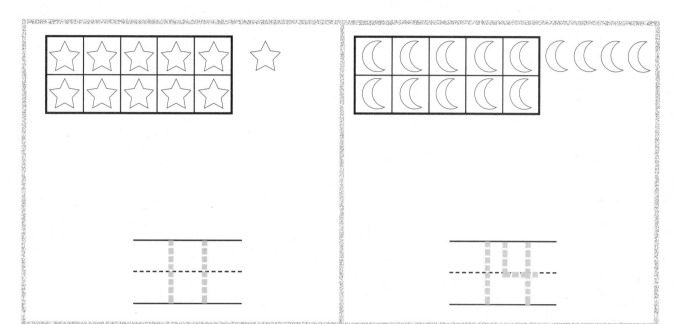

1. Count. Write the number.

2.

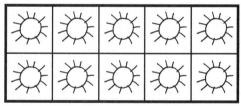

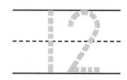

_____
_____
_____

3. Choose two numbers from 10 through 15.

Draw pictures to show each number.

Use with text pages 17–18.

Name _____ Date _____

Activity: Numbers 16 Through 20

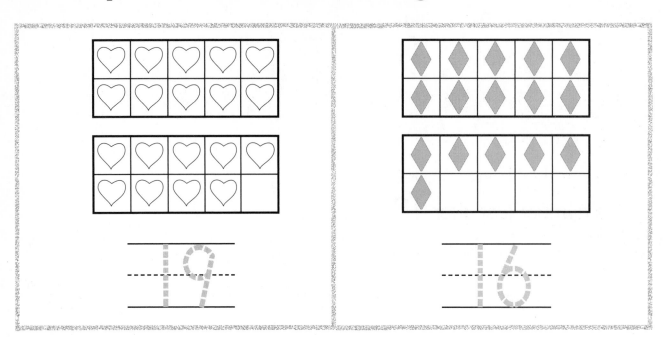

Count. Write the number.

1.

2.

3. Choose a number from
16 through 20.

Draw a picture to show
the number.

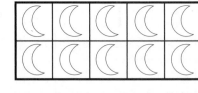

Use with text pages 19–20.

Order 11 Through 20

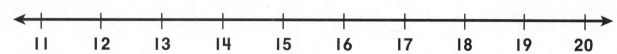

11 12 13 14 15 16 17 18 19 20

> You can use a number line to order numbers.
>
> The number just before 17 is _____.
>
> The number between 12 and 14 is _____.
>
> The number just after 18 is _____.

Use the number line. Write the number.

Just Before	Between	Just After
1. _____ , 18	11, _____ , 13	11, _____
2. _____ , 14	17, _____ , 19	19, _____

3. Choose two numbers from 11 through 20.

Write your numbers in the chart.

Write the numbers before and after your numbers.

The Number Before	My Number	The Number After

Use with text pages 21–22.

7

Compare 11 Through 20

You can compare numbers using the words greater than, less than, and equal to.

Circle the words that make the sentence true.

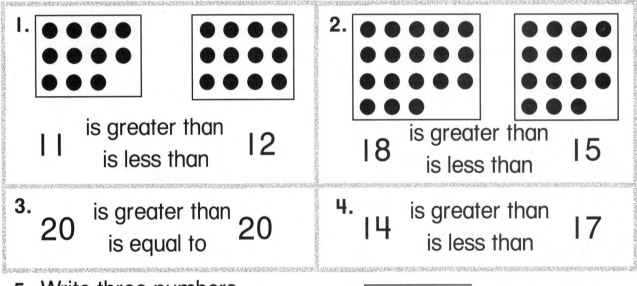

5. Write three numbers that are greater than 12 but less than 20.

_____
- - - - - - - - - - -
_____
_____
- - - - - - - - - - -
_____
_____
- - - - - - - - - - -
_____

Use with text pages 23–24.

Problem Solving:
Draw a Picture

Jackie has 4 hats. Josh has 1 more hat than Jackie.
How many hats does Josh have?

What do I know?

Jackie has _____ hats.

Josh has _____ more hat
than Jackie.

Plan

Start with Jackie's hats.

Jackie has _____ hats.

Solve

Draw Jackie's hats.

Draw 1 more hat to show
Josh's hats.

Josh has _____ hats.

Draw here.

Look Back

Does my answer make sense?

Use with text pages 25–27.

Name _____ Date _____

Activity: Addition Stories

There are 3 white dogs. There are 2 black dogs.
Show the story with small items such as buttons,
coins, or macaroni.

Count the items you have and write the numbers.

___3___   ___2___   ___5___ in all

Write the numbers.

1. There are 4 ladybugs on a leaf.
   Then 1 ladybug joins them.

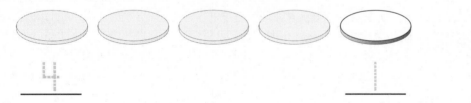

___4___   ___1___   ___5___ in all

2. Make up a story of your own.
   Write the numbers in your story.

   _____   _____   _____

Use with text pages 35–36.

Model Addition

You add the parts to find the whole.

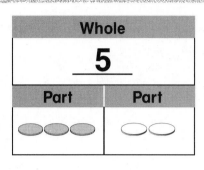

Use small items such as buttons or coins to show the parts. Write the whole.

1. Dalia has 1 balloon.
   A clown gave her 1 more.

Whole	
2	
Part	Part
_____	_____

2. Iris had 1 ball. She found 2 more.

Whole	
_____	
Part	Part
_____	_____

3. Look in your room to find things you have in 2 different colors. For example, 3 green baseball caps and 3 red caps. Show your story.

Use with text pages 37–38.

Name _____ Date _____

Use Symbols to Add

You can use symbols to write an addition sentence.

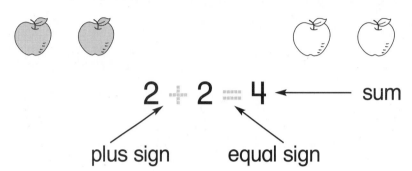

2 + 2 = 4 ← sum

plus sign   equal sign

Write the sum.

1.

3   +   1   = ___

2.

4   +   2   = ___

3. Circle the picture that shows $2 + 3 = 5$.

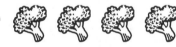

Use with text pages 39–40.

12

Add With Zero

> When you add zero to a number, the sum is the number.
>
>
>
> 3 + 0 = 3

Write the sum.

1. $2 + 0 =$ __2__   2. $3 + 1 =$ ____

3. $0 + 7 =$ ____   4. $0 + 4 =$ ____

5. $6 + 0 =$ ____   6. $5 + 1 =$ ____

7. $2 + 2 =$ ____   8. $0 + 0 =$ ____

9. Tell a story in which nothing is added to a certain number of things. Draw pictures to show your story. Write an addition sentence to show the sum.

____ $+ 0 =$ ____

Use with text pages 41–42.

Add in Any Order

Look at the balloons.

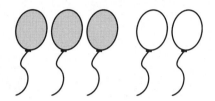   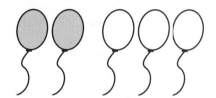

$$3 + 2 = 5 \qquad\qquad 2 + 3 = 5$$

You can change the order of the addends and get the same sum.

Add. Then change the order of the addends and add.

1. $2 + 1 = $ _____

   ___ $+$ ___ $= 3$

2. $4 + 2 = $ _____

   ___ $+$ ___ $= $ _____

3. $1 + 4 = $ _____

   ___ $+$ ___ $= $ _____

4. $0 + 6 = $ _____

   ___ $+$ ___ $= $ _____

5. $1 + 5 = $ _____

   ___ $+$ ___ $= $ _____

6. $3 + 2 = $ _____

   ___ $+$ ___ $= $ _____

7. Amy has 2 pens. John gives her 5 more pens. Write two addition sentences to show how many pens Amy has in all.

Draw or write to explain.

Use with text pages 45–46.

Ways to Make Numbers

There are different ways to make 7. Here is one way.

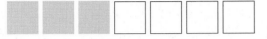

$$3 + 4 = 7$$

Here is another way.

$$2 + 5 = 7$$

There are different ways to make 8. Here is one way.

$$5 + 3 = 8$$

Here is another way.

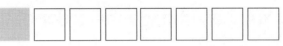

$$1 + 7 = 8$$

Use two colors to show a way to make 7.
Complete the addition sentence.

1.

_____ + _____ = _____

Use two colors to show a way to make 8.
Complete the addition sentence.

2.

_____ + _____ = _____

3.

_____ + _____ = _____

Use with text pages 47–48.

Name _____ Date _____

Homework
2.7

Add in Vertical Form

You can write the same addition fact in two ways.

You can add across.   You can add down.

$$3 + 2 = 5$$

$$\begin{array}{r} 3 \\ +2 \\ \hline 5 \end{array}$$

Write the sum.

1. $\begin{array}{r} 4 \\ +2 \\ \hline 6 \end{array}$
2. $\begin{array}{r} 5 \\ +1 \\ \hline \end{array}$
3. $\begin{array}{r} 8 \\ +0 \\ \hline \end{array}$
4. $\begin{array}{r} 3 \\ +3 \\ \hline \end{array}$
5. $\begin{array}{r} 2 \\ +1 \\ \hline \end{array}$

6. $\begin{array}{r} 4 \\ +0 \\ \hline \end{array}$
7. $\begin{array}{r} 7 \\ +1 \\ \hline \end{array}$
8. $\begin{array}{r} 2 \\ +5 \\ \hline \end{array}$
9. $\begin{array}{r} 1 \\ +6 \\ \hline \end{array}$
10. $\begin{array}{r} 3 \\ +5 \\ \hline \end{array}$

11. Find two different items in your home you can add together. Add the two numbers. Show your addition across and up and down.

Draw or write here.

Copyright © Houghton Mifflin Company. All rights reserved.

Use with text pages 49–50.

16

Name _____ Date _____

Problem Solving:
Write a Number Sentence

One step in solving an addition problem
is to write a number sentence.

Melissa has **3** trading cards.

Jeff has **5** trading cards.

$$3 + 5 = 8$$

Write a number sentence.

1. There are **5** kangaroos in the grass. **2** more kangaroos join them. How many kangaroos are there?

_____ kangaroos

2. There are **6** koala bears. **2** more join them. How many koala bears are there?

_____ koala bears

Use with text pages 51–53.

Activity: Subtraction Stories

Paul had 4 balloons.

He gave 2 balloons to Brad.

Use buttons or coins to show the story and write the numbers.

___4___ ___2___ given away   ___2___ left

Use buttons or coins to show the story and write the numbers.

1. Emily had 5 balls. She lost
   one. How many balls does
   she have left?

   _____ balls _____ lost _____ left

   Draw here.

2. You have 5 books and take
   2 to school. How many books
   do you have left?

   _____ books _____ to school _____ left

   Draw here.

Use with text pages 61–62.

Name _____ Date _____

Model Subtraction

If you know the whole and one of the parts, you can subtract to find the other part.

There are 5 buttons in all. 3 buttons are in one part. How many are in the other part?

Whole	
5	
Part	Part
3	___

Use counters.

Show the whole.

Move the counters to the one part. Find the other part.

1.

Whole	
3	
Part	Part
2	___

2.

Whole	
5	
Part	Part
2	___

3.

Whole	
4	
Part	Part
3	___

4.

Whole	
4	
Part	Part
1	___

Draw a set with 1 fewer.

5.

Use with text pages 63–64.

Name _____ Date _____

Use Symbols to Subtract

You can use a minus sign and an equal sign to write about subtraction.

$$5 \quad - \quad 2 \quad = \quad 3$$

minus sign   equal sign

You can circle and cross out to show subtraction.

Circle and cross out to subtract.

Write how many are left.

1.

$$4 - 2 = \underline{\quad}$$

2.

$$3 - 2 = \underline{\quad}$$

3.

$$6 - 4 = \underline{\quad}$$

4.

$$5 - 2 = \underline{\quad}$$

5. Circle the picture that shows $4 - 3$.

Use with text pages 65–66.

Write Subtraction Sentences

You can write a subtraction sentence
to show the difference.

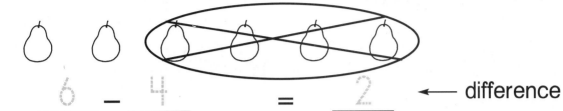

_6_ – _4_ = _2_ ← difference

The difference tells how many are left.

Write the subtraction sentence.

1.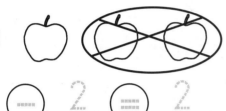

_4_ ⊖ _2_ ⊜ _2_

2.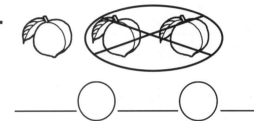

___ ◯ ___ ◯ ___

Write the difference.

3. 4 – 1 = ____

4. 5 – 2 = ____

5. 6 – 4 = ____

6. 2 – 1 = ____

7. Solve the problem.

I am less than 4.
I am greater than 1.
I am not 2.
What number am I?

Draw or write to explain.

____

Use with text pages 67–68.

Zero in Subtraction

When you subtract zero from a number, you get the number.

$4 - 0 = \underline{4}$

When you subtract a number from itself, you get zero.

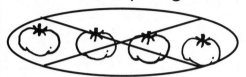

$4 - 4 = \underline{0}$

Write the difference.

1.

$3 - 3 = \underline{0}$

2.

$5 - 0 = \underline{}$

3.

$2 - 0 = \underline{}$

4.

$4 - 4 = \underline{}$

5. $6 - 6 = \underline{}$

6. $4 - 0 = \underline{}$

7. $1 - 0 = \underline{}$

8. $3 - 3 = \underline{}$

9. Tony has 6 flowers.
He gives away 6 flowers.
Write the difference.

$6 - 6 = \underline{}$

Draw to explain.

Use with text pages 71–72.

Name _____ Date _____

Subtract From 8 or Less

You can subtract from **8** or less.

Use **7** paper clips. Circle and cross out **2**. Write the subtraction sentence.

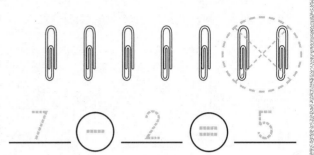

$$\underline{7} - \bigcirc \underline{2} \bigcirc \underline{5}$$

Use paper clips. Take away some.
Circle and cross out.
Write the subtraction sentence.

Use **7** paper clips.

1. _____ ⃝ _____ ⃝ _____

2. _____ ⃝ _____ ⃝ _____

Use **8** paper clips.

3. _____ ⃝ _____ ⃝ _____

4. _____ ⃝ _____ ⃝ _____

Write the subtraction sentence.

5. Shanna has **7** books. She gave **3** books to her sister. How many books does she have left?

_____ ⃝ _____ ⃝ _____

Draw or write to explain.

Use with text pages 73–74.

Name _____ Date _____

Subtract in Vertical Form

You can write the same subtraction fact in two ways.
The difference is the same.

Subtract across.   Subtract down.

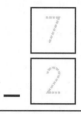

___7___ – ___2___ = ___5___ ←difference   5   ← difference

Complete the subtraction fact.

1.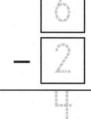

___6___ – ___2___ = ___4___

2.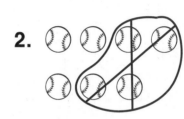

_____ – _____ = _____

3.

_____ – _____ = _____

4.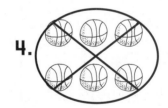

_____ – _____ = _____

5. Complete the subtraction fact.

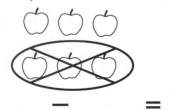

_____ – _____ = _____

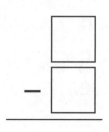

Use with text pages 75–76.

Name _____ Date _____

Problem Solving:
Act It Out With Models

Use models to act out subtraction problems.

There are 5 birds.

3 birds fly away.

How many birds are left?

To model the problem,

show 5 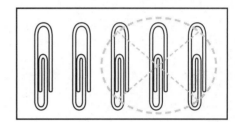 for birds.

Now take away 3.

Count how many are left.

There are ___2___ birds left.

Draw the problem. Write the answer. | **Draw or write to explain.**

1. David has 2 hot dogs. He eats
   1 hot dog. How many hot dogs
   does he have left?

   _____ hot dog

2. Orlee has 6 dolls. She gives
   3 dolls away. How many dolls
   does she have left?

   _____ dolls

3. Jenny has 8 flowers. She gives
   5 away. How many flowers
   does she have left?

   _____ flowers

Use with text pages 77–79.

Activity: Make a Tally Chart

Mr. Sanchez wanted to see how many toys he had in his store.

Look at the tally chart.

Each | stands for 1 toy.

Each ⽕ stands for 5.

There were 3 dolls in his store.

There were 5 robots.

Toys	
🧑	|||
🤖	⽕

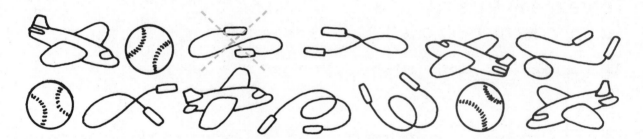

1. Cross out one item and write a tally mark in the chart. Repeat until you complete the tally chart.

Toys	
🪢	
⚾	
✈	

2. Choose 3 things in the kitchen that have more than one item. For example: forks, chairs, or pots. Make your own tally chart.

Things in the kitchen	

Use with text pages 87–88.

Read a Pictograph

A pictograph uses pictures to show information.
Each 🌸 stands for 1 animal.

Here is a pictograph that shows how many lions and elephants there are in the zoo.

More Animals in the Zoo

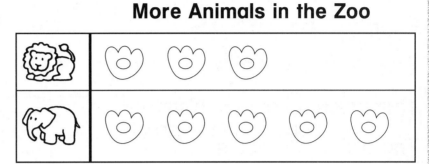

There are 3 lions and 5 elephants in the zoo.

More Animals in the Zoo

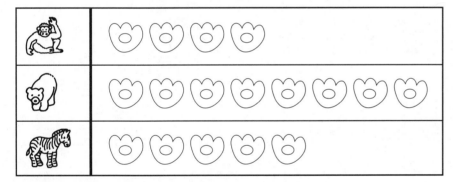

Use the pictograph to solve.
Each 🌸 stands for 1 animal.

1. Which animal does the zoo have the most of? Circle.

2. How many zebras are there? _____ zebras

3. How many bears are there?

_____ bears

Use with text pages 89–90.

Make a Pictograph

You can make a pictograph.

For each picture you cross out, draw a ⌒ in the graph.

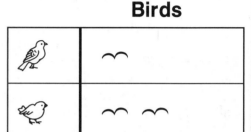

The child who is making this graph has just begun.
She needs to put **3** more robins and
4 more sparrows in the graph.

Birds

🐦	⌒
🐤	⌒ ⌒

1. Use the picture.
   Make a pictograph.
   Show how many.

Birds

🦆	
🐔	

Use the pictograph to solve.

2. How many 🦆 are there?

_____

3. How many 🐔 are there?

_____

4. How many more 🐔 than
   🦆 are there? _____

5. How many 🦆 and 🐔 are
   there in all? _____

Use with text pages 91–93.

Read a Bar Graph

This is a bar graph.

It tells how many kinds of dogs

are in the animal hospital.

Each box on the graph stands for one kind of dog.

There are 7 🐑 .

Dogs in the Animal Hospital								
🐑								
🐕								
🐶								
0	1	2	3	4	5	6	7	8

Number of Dogs

Use the bar graph. Solve.

1. How many are there?

   5
   _____

2. Are there fewer or

   ? Circle.

3. How many more 🐶 are

   there than 🐕?

   _____ more

4. What kind of dog is there

   the most of? Circle.

   🐶   🐑   🐕

Use with text pages 95–96.

Activity: Make a Bar Graph

You can use a tally chart to make a bar graph.

There are 4 tallies in the first row.

There are 4 boxes shaded in the first row.

There are 4 of the first kind of kite.

Kites at the Fair

(kite)	IIII
(box kite)	II
(star kite)	IIII

Kites at the Fair

	0	1	2	3	4	5	6
(kite)							
(box kite)							
(star kite)							

Number of Kites

Use the tally chart to complete the bar graph.

1.

Kites

(bird kite)	IIII
(flower kite)	III
(butterfly kite)	IIII

More Kites at the Fair

	0	1	2	3	4	5	6
(bird kite)							
(flower kite)							
(butterfly kite)							

Number of Kites

2. You have different colored socks in a drawer. How can you show how many socks of each color you have?

Draw or write to explain.

Use with text pages 97–99.

Problem Solving: Use a Graph

This graph shows how many cars are in a parking lot.
Use the graph to solve.

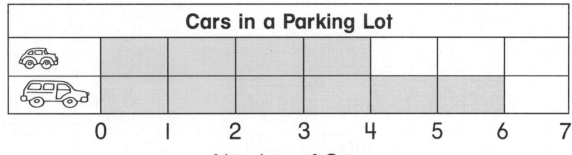

How many small cars are there?

___4___ small cars

Use the graph to solve.

1. How many big cars are there?

___6___ big cars

2. How many cars are there in all?

_____ cars

3. How many more big cars than small cars are there?

_____ more

4. 3 more small cars drive into the parking lot. Fill in boxes to show 3 more small cars. How many more small cars are there now?

_____ small car

Use with text pages 101–103.

Name _____ Date _____

Count On to Add

You can count on to add.
Find $5 + 3$.

Start with 5. Count on 3.

$\boxed{5}$, $\underline{6}$, $\underline{7}$, $\underline{8}$ $5 + 3 = 8$

Count on to add.

1. $4 + 2 = \underline{6}$	2. $1 + 2 = \underline{}$	3. $4 + 3 = \underline{}$
4. $\begin{array}{r} 3 \\ +2 \\ \hline \end{array}$	5. $\begin{array}{r} 6 \\ +2 \\ \hline \end{array}$	6. $\begin{array}{r} 2 \\ +5 \\ \hline \end{array}$
7. $\begin{array}{r} 8 \\ +1 \\ \hline \end{array}$	8. $\begin{array}{r} 3 \\ +5 \\ \hline \end{array}$	9. $\begin{array}{r} 4 \\ +1 \\ \hline \end{array}$

10. You have 4 new yellow pencils. Count on to add 3 red pencils. How many pencils do you have in all?

Draw or write to explain.

_____ pencils

Use with text pages 125–126.

Use a Number Line to Add

You can use a number line to add.
Find $5 + 2$.
Start with 5 on the number line.
Count on 2 more numbers.

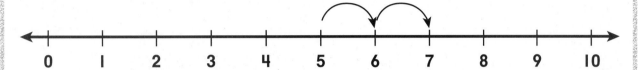

You end on 7.

$5 + 2 = \underline{\quad 7 \quad}$

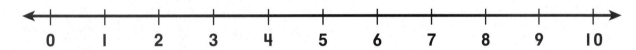

Find the sum.

1. $5 + 3 = \underline{\quad 8 \quad}$

2. $2 + 5 = \underline{\quad\quad}$

3. $\begin{array}{r} 6 \\ + 3 \\ \hline \end{array}$

4. $\begin{array}{r} 4 \\ + 2 \\ \hline \end{array}$

5. $\begin{array}{r} 3 \\ + 5 \\ \hline \end{array}$

6. $\begin{array}{r} 2 \\ + 6 \\ \hline \end{array}$

7. Choose two of the numbers below. Write an addition problem. Use a number line to solve.

| 6 | 2 | 3 |

Draw or write to explain.

Use with text pages 127–128.

Use Doubles to Add

You can use doubles to add.
This is a double.

3 + 3 = 6

addend addend sum

A doubles fact has two
addends that are the same.

2 + 2 = 4

addend addend sum

Write the sum.

1. 1 + 1 = ___2___

2. 5 + 5 = _____

3. 3
   + 3
   ___

4. 2
   + 2
   ___

5. 1
   + 1
   ___

6. 4
   + 4
   ___

7. 4 children are playing in the park. 4 more children join them. How many children are there in all?

4 + 4 = _____

8. There are 5 children playing in the park. Then 5 more children join them. How many children are there in all?

5 + 5 = _____

Use with text pages 129–131.

Using Addition Strategies

Ways to add

Count on.   Use counters.

Use a number line.   Use doubles.

Draw a picture.

Choose a way to add. Find the sum.

1. $\begin{array}{r} 3 \\ +\,6 \\ \hline \end{array}$
   9

2. $\begin{array}{r} 1 \\ +\,6 \\ \hline \end{array}$

3. $\begin{array}{r} 5 \\ +\,5 \\ \hline \end{array}$

4. $\begin{array}{r} 5 \\ +\,4 \\ \hline \end{array}$

5. $\begin{array}{r} 2 \\ +\,4 \\ \hline \end{array}$

6. $\begin{array}{r} 3 \\ +\,3 \\ \hline \end{array}$

7. $\begin{array}{r} 3 \\ +\,5 \\ \hline \end{array}$

8. $\begin{array}{r} 7 \\ +\,1 \\ \hline \end{array}$

9. $7 + 2 =$ _____

10. $4 + 5 =$ _____

Choose two ways to solve the problem.

11. There are 6 flowers in the vase. Then 1 more is added. How many flowers are there in all?

Draw or write to explain.

_____ flowers

Use with text pages 133–134.

Problem Solving:
Write a Number Sentence

You can use a sentence to solve a problem.

2 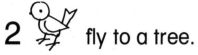 fly to a tree.

6 more  fly to the tree.

How many 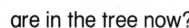 are in the tree now?

_2_ (+) _6_ (=) _8_

---

1. There are 4 black ants and 5 red ants. How many ants are there in all?

_4_ (+) _5_ (=) _9_

_9_ ants

---

2. Dalia has 6 crayons. Amit has 2 crayons. How many crayons do they have in all?

___ ( ) ___ ( ) ___

___ crayons

---

3. There are 3 girls and 4 boys at the party. How many children are at the party?

___ ( ) ___ ( ) ___

___ children

Use with text pages 135–137.

Count Back to Subtract

You can count back to subtract.
Find $7 - 3$.
Here's how you count back from 7.

$$\boxed{7}, \quad 6, \quad 5, \quad 4$$

When you count 3 back from 7, you end on 4.

$$7 - 3 = 4$$

Count back to subtract.

1. $4 - 2 =$ __2__

2. $7 - 1 =$ ____

3. $5 - 1 =$ ____

4. $10 - 2 =$ ____

5. $\begin{array}{r} 8 \\ -2 \\ \hline \end{array}$

6. $\begin{array}{r} 2 \\ -1 \\ \hline \end{array}$

7. $\begin{array}{r} 5 \\ -2 \\ \hline \end{array}$

8. $\begin{array}{r} 9 \\ -3 \\ \hline \end{array}$

9. You have 8 grapes. You want to give 3 to your friend. How many will you have left?

Count back to subtract.

$\boxed{8}$ ____, ____, ____

____ grapes left

Use with text pages 145–146.

Name _____ Date _____

Use a Number Line to Subtract

Find $7 - 2$.
You can use a number line to subtract.
Start at 7. Count back 2.

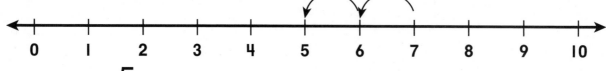

You end on 5.

$$7 - 2 = 5$$

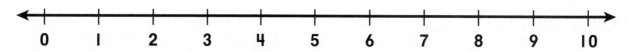

Use the number line to find the difference.

1. $6 - 3 = \underline{}$

2. $4 - 2 = \underline{}$

3. $7 - 1 = \underline{}$

4. $9 - 2 = \underline{}$

5.
$$\begin{array}{r} 5 \\ -\ 2 \\ \hline \end{array}$$

6.
$$\begin{array}{r} 8 \\ -\ 2 \\ \hline \end{array}$$

7.
$$\begin{array}{r} 4 \\ -\ 1 \\ \hline \end{array}$$

8.
$$\begin{array}{r} 9 \\ -\ 3 \\ \hline \end{array}$$

Read. Then draw to solve.

9. There are 5 birds.
   3 birds fly away.
   How many birds
   are left?

   Draw here.

   _____ birds

Use with text pages 147–148.

How Many More?
How Many Fewer?

To compare numbers, subtract.

How many more  than 🐱 are there?

Match each 🐱 to one 🐕. Then subtract.

$6 - 3 = 3$ There are 3 more dogs than cats.

Match. Then subtract.

1. How many more ◯
than △ are there?

$7 - 2 =$ _____

◯◯◯◯◯◯◯

△△

2. How many fewer ◇
than ▢ are there?

$8 - 3 =$ _____

▢▢▢▢▢▢▢

◇ ◇ ◇

3. How many fewer △ than
◯ are there?

$9 - 4 =$ _____

◯◯◯◯◯◯◯◯◯

△△△△

Use with text pages 149–151.

Relate Addition and Subtraction

Three different numbers can make both an addition and a subtraction sentence.

These addition and subtraction facts have the same parts and wholes. They are related facts.

Whole
8

Part	Part
5	3

$5 + 3 = 8 \quad 8 - 3 = 5$

Use pennies. Show the parts. Then complete the related facts.

1. $5 + 3 =$ ____

$8 - 3 =$ ____

2. $6 + 2 =$ ____

$8 - 2 =$ ____

3. $8 + 1 =$ ____

$9 - 1 =$ ____

4. Make up a story.
Use the numbers
7 and 2 in the story.
Write an addition sentence
that goes with your story.
Then write a related
subtraction sentence.

____ + ____ = ____

____ − ____ = ____

Use with text pages 153–154.

Name _____ Date _____

Fact Families

Related facts make a fact family.

8 is the whole. **2** and **6** are the parts.

$$2 + 6 = 8 \qquad 8 - 6 = 2$$
$$6 + 2 = 8 \qquad 8 - 2 = 6$$

Complete the fact family.

1.

Whole	
9	
Part	Part
7	2

$7 + \underline{\ 2\ } = \underline{\ 9\ }$
$2 + \underline{\ \ \ } = \underline{\ \ \ }$
$9 - \underline{\ \ \ } = \underline{\ \ \ }$
$9 - \underline{\ \ \ } = \underline{\ \ \ }$

2.

Whole	
7	
Part	Part
3	4

$\underline{\ \ \ } + \underline{\ \ \ } = \underline{\ \ \ }$
$\underline{\ \ \ } + \underline{\ \ \ } = \underline{\ \ \ }$
$\underline{\ \ \ } - \underline{\ \ \ } = \underline{\ \ \ }$
$\underline{\ \ \ } - \underline{\ \ \ } = \underline{\ \ \ }$

Solve.

3. Liz has **6** farm animals. **4** are chickens. **2** are pigs. Use the numbers to complete a fact family.

$\underline{\ \ \ } + \underline{\ \ \ } = \underline{\ \ \ }$
$\underline{\ \ \ } + \underline{\ \ \ } = \underline{\ \ \ }$
$\underline{\ \ \ } - \underline{\ \ \ } = \underline{\ \ \ }$
$\underline{\ \ \ } - \underline{\ \ \ } = \underline{\ \ \ }$

Use with text pages 155–156.

Name _____ Date _____

Using Subtraction Strategies

There are different ways to subtract $5 - 3$.

You can count back. , 4, 3, 2

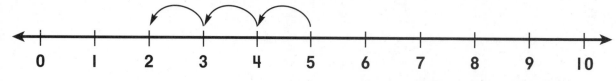

You can draw a picture.

You can use a related
addition fact.

$3 + 2 = 5$
$5 - 3 = 2$

Choose a way to subtract. Write the difference.

1. $7 - 2 =$ ___

2. $8 - 1 =$ ___

3. $6 - 5 =$ ___

4. $7 - 4 =$ ___

5. $6 - 3 =$ ___

6. $9 - 5 =$ ___

7. $10 - 2 =$ ___

8. $4 - 2 =$ ___

Draw and write. Use more paper if you need it.

9. Make up a subtraction story.
   Tell someone two ways you can
   solve the problem in your story.

Use with text pages 157–158.

Name _____ Date _____

Problem Solving:
Choose the Operation

You can add or subtract to solve a problem.

Choose the operation to solve.

Draw or write to explain.

1. 6 children are at the park.
2 go home.
How many children are left?

_____ children

2. 5 children are playing
soccer. 3 more join them.
How many children are
there now?

_____ children

3. 7 children are in school.
5 go home.
How many children are left?

_____ children

Use with text pages 159–161.

Classifying and Sorting Objects

You can sort objects by color, size, or shape.

Tell how the objects are alike.
Write color, size, or shape.

1.

SHAPE
_____

2.

_____

3.

_____

4. Find 3 socks. Draw them.
   How are they alike?
   How are they different?

Draw here.

Use with text pages 183–184.

Plane Shapes

Plane shapes are flat.
Some plane shapes have
straight sides.

square   rectangle   triangle

Some plane shapes are round.

circle

1. Color red the shapes with
   3 sides.

2. Color black the shapes with
   no sides.

3. Color blue the shapes with
   the **4** sides the same.

4. Color green the shapes with
   4 sides not the same.

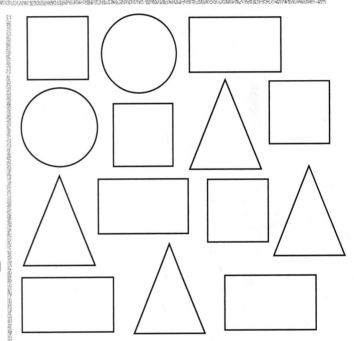

5. Draw an object using plane
   shapes. How many shapes
   did you use?

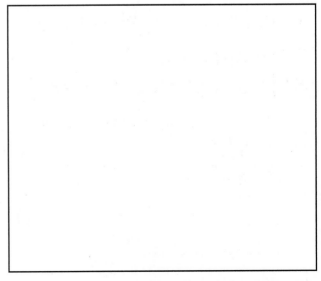

Use with text pages 185–186.

Name _____ Date _____

Classifying and Sorting Shapes

You can sort shapes in many ways.

Some shapes have 3 or 4 corners.

Some shapes have 3 or 4 sides.

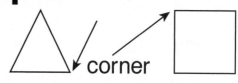
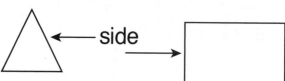

Circle the shapes that follow the rule.

1. 3 sides

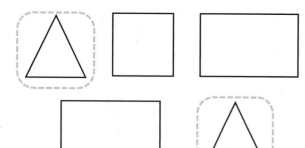

2. 4 sides the same

3. More than 3 sides

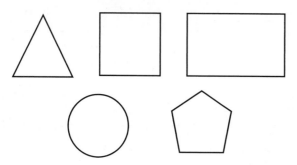

4. No corners

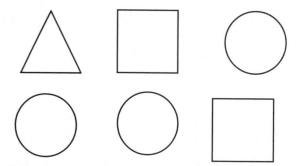

5. Draw a picture of shapes that follow the rule. Shapes with 4 corners.

Draw here.

Use with text pages 187–188.

Name _____ Date _____

Activity: Solid Shapes

Solid shapes have special names.

cube   **cone**   **sphere**   **rectangular   prism**   **pyramid**   **cylinder**

Solids can move.

Roll   Slide   Stack

Find how each solid can move.
Complete the table.

		Slide	Stack	Roll
1.	SOAP			
2.	SOUP			
3.	(baseball)			

4. Duncan has a shape with 6 faces and 12 edges. Not all the faces are the same. Circle the shape he made.

cube rectangular prism pyramid

Draw or write to explain.

Use with text pages 191–192.

Classifying and Sorting Solid Shapes

You can sort solid shapes many ways.

6 faces   Curved parts   5 corners

Look at the picture below. Then sort the
solid shapes according to the rule.

1. Draw a line under the shapes with 0 faces.

2. Circle the shapes with 6 faces.

3. Draw a box around the shapes with 1 face.

4. Draw an X through the shapes with 2 faces.

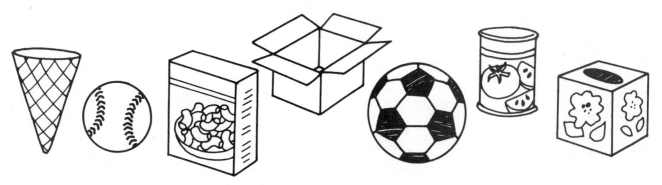

5. Look in your kitchen. Draw
   a solid shape that can roll.

Draw here.

Use with text pages 193–194.

Name _____ Date _____

Identify Faces of a Solid Shape

The face of a solid is a plane shape. The face is flat.

triangle   **square**   **rectangle**   **circle**

Look at the plane shape. Circle the solid with a face like it.

1.

2.

3.

4.

5. Lisa traced two solid shapes to make this shape. Circle the solid shapes she used.

cube   pyramid   cylinder

sphere   rectangular prism

Use with text pages 195–196.

Problem Solving Strategy:
Draw a Picture

Sometimes a picture can help you solve a problem.
Draw a picture to solve.

	Draw.
1. Stella wants to make a clown face with a pointed hat. Which shapes should she use? □ ○ △	
2. Rory has cut paper in these shapes: △ ▭ ○ How can he make a tree?	
3. Lyle wants to use shapes to draw a snowman. Show how he can do it.	
4. Nina wants to draw a wagon with these shapes: ⏢ ○ ▯ Show how she can do it.	

Use with text pages 197–199.

Name _____ Date _____

Position Words

Some position words are **over,**
under, between, left, and **right.**

Complete the sentence using **over,**
under, between, left, and **right.**

1. The 🐕 is __under__ the

tree.

2. The 🧒 is to the

_____ of the 🌳.

3. The ☀️ is _____ the

tree.

4. The 🤸 is to the _____

of the tree.

5. The 🌳 is _____

the girl and the boy.

6. Locate the chair you are
sitting on using the words
over, under, between,
left, and **right.**

Draw or write to explain.

Use with text pages 207–208.

Name _____ Date _____

More Position Words

You can use more position words to tell where things are.
Some of these words are **behind, in front of, far from,
next to, near, up,** and **down.**

Circle the answer that completes the sentence.

1. The cat goes

_____ the stairs.

up, down

2. The rabbit is

_____ the carrot.

far from, near

3. The mountain is

_____ the cloud.

in front of, behind

4. The baby is _____

the carriage.

next to, far from

Talk About It   Tell the location of objects near your bed.
Use all the position words from this page.

Use with text pages 209–210.

Name _____ Date _____

Give and Follow Directions

This grid shows places in the garden.

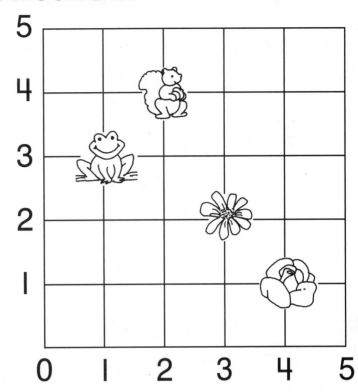

Follow the directions.

Circle the flower or animal you find.

1. Go right 3 spaces. Go up 2 spaces. What do you find?

2. Go right 2 spaces. Go up 4 spaces. What do you find?

3. Go right 4 spaces. Go up 1 space. What do you find?

4. Go right 1 space. Go up 3 spaces. What do you find?

5. Draw a flower on the grid. Write where the flower is.

_____ spaces to the right

_____ spaces up

Use with text pages 211–212.

Name _____ Date _____

Homework 8.4

Activity: Slides, Flips, and Turns

You can move an object different ways.
You can flip it, turn it, or slide it.

Flip   **Turn**   **Slide**

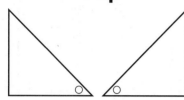 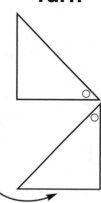 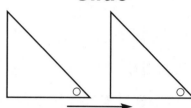

Draw the shape to show a turn.   Draw the shape to show a flip.

1. 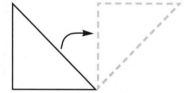   **2.**

Draw the shape to show a slide.

3.

4. Cut out a shape like this. Trace the
shape. Move the shape to show a flip,
a turn, and a slide.

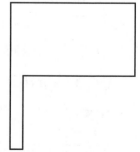

Copyright © Houghton Mifflin Company. All rights reserved.

Use with text pages 215–218.

Name _____ Date _____

Patterns

You can make a pattern with shapes.

This is a square, circle, square, circle,
square, circle pattern.
Circle the shape that comes next.

Draw the shape that comes next.

I.

2.

3.

4.

5. Draw a pattern for beads using **2** shapes.

Use with text pages 219–220.

Name _____ Date _____

Create Patterns

You can create a pattern using shapes.

Tanisha made a pattern for beads. She put
them on a string. Circle the pattern unit.

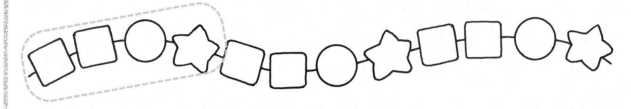

Use these shapes to make a pattern unit.
Draw a pattern on a separate sheet of paper.

1.

2.

3. **A   M   T**

4. Draw a pattern unit with **3** shapes. Draw the pattern unit two
   more times to make a pattern. Ask someone which shape
   comes next.

Use with text pages 221–222.

Translate Patterns

You can show the same kind of pattern in more than one way.

Find the pattern. Draw shapes to show it another way.

1.

2.

3. Look at the pattern.

   Use words to describe how you could draw the pattern another way.

   ○ ○ □ ○ ○ □

   _____
   _____
   _____

Use with text pages 223–224.

Name _____ Date _____

Symmetry

Some shapes have symmetry. They have **2** matching parts.

Some shapes do not have symmetry. They have no matching parts.

Draw a line of symmetry.
Remember, the **2** parts must match.

1.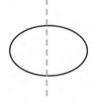

2.

3.

4.

5. The shape has **2** lines of symmetry. Draw the **2** lines of symmetry.

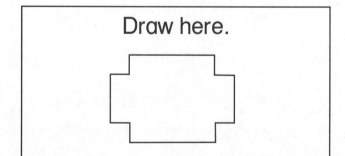

Draw here.

Use with text pages 225–227.

Problem Solving:
Find a Pattern

Read It Look for information.

Kivi is making a picture frame. Here is the pattern.
What shape comes next?

Say It Say the pattern unit.

Write It Write the pattern unit with words.

_____ _____ _____

Solve It Use the pattern unit to solve.

1. Say what shape comes next in the pattern.

2. Circle the shape that comes next.

Use with text pages 229–231.

Equal Parts

Some whole shapes can be divided into equal parts.

Equal parts are the same size.

whole

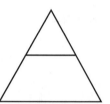

equal parts

1. Circle the shape that shows equal parts.

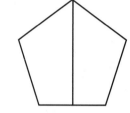

Write the number of equal parts.

2.

_____ equal parts

3.
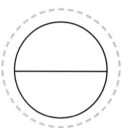

_____ equal parts

4.

_____ equal parts

5.

_____ equal parts

6. Draw to show how you would slice a pizza into 4 equal parts.

Draw here.

Use with text pages 239–240.

One Half

You can use a fraction to name equal parts.

The rectangle shows two halves.

One half of the rectangle is gray. The other half is white.

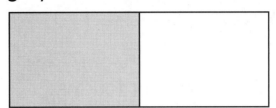

$\dfrac{1}{2}$ $\dfrac{1}{2}$ $\dfrac{1}{2}$ gray $\dfrac{1}{2}$ white

Color $\dfrac{1}{2}$.

1.
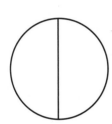

2.

Draw a line to show halves.

3.

4.
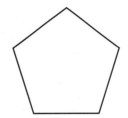

5. Look at an open book or magazine. Does it form two halves? Find things at home that have two halves. Draw what you find.

Use with text pages 241–242.

One Fourth

One fourth is a fraction that names part of a whole.

| $\frac{1}{4}$ | $\frac{1}{4}$ | $\frac{1}{4}$ | $\frac{1}{4}$ |

There are **4** equal parts.
There are four fourths.

| $\frac{1}{4}$ | $\frac{1}{4}$ | $\frac{1}{4}$ | $\frac{1}{4}$ |

1 out of **4** parts is gray.
$\frac{1}{4}$ is gray.

Color $\frac{1}{4}$.

1.

2.

Draw lines to show fourths.
Color $\frac{1}{4}$.

3.

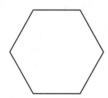

4.

5. Find a shape that you can make into **3** parts. Draw lines to show thirds. Color **1** part.

Use with text pages 243–244.

Name _____ Date _____

Fractions of a Set

You can use a fraction to name a part of a set.

$\dfrac{1}{4}$ part is gray
       parts in all

Circle the fraction that names the gray part.

1.

$\dfrac{1}{2}$ $\dfrac{1}{3}$ $\left(\dfrac{1}{4}\right)$

2.

$\dfrac{1}{2}$ $\dfrac{1}{3}$ $\dfrac{1}{4}$

Color to show the fraction.

3. $\dfrac{1}{2}$

4. $\dfrac{1}{4}$

5. Carlos has **3** birds. Draw the birds. $\dfrac{1}{3}$ of them are yellow. Color to show the fraction.

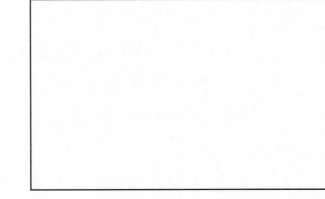

Use with text pages 247–248.

Activity: Probability

When you predict, you tell what may happen.

There are more in the jar than .

So, it is more likely that you would pick a .

How likely is it that you will pick a star? Circle.

1.

more likely   equally likely   ~~less likely~~

2.

more likely   equally likely   less likely

3.

more likely   equally likely   less likely

4.

more likely   equally likely   less likely

5. Draw any number of Xs and Zs in the jar. Are you more likely or less likely to pick an X or a Z?

_____ likely

Draw here.

Use with text pages 249–250.

Problem Solving: Use a Picture

You can use a picture to predict the chance of something happening.

Danni is going to pick a prize from the bag.

He is more likely to pick a horn because there are more horns to pick.

1. Izzi asks Sandy to pick a prize. Which prize is she more likely to pick?

2. Gale closes her eyes to pick a treat. Which is she less likely to pick?

3. Rosa has socks in a drawer. How many more gray socks are there than white socks?

_____ more gray socks

4. Keb asks Tani to pick a treat. Which treat is Tani more likely to pick?

5. Sal puts 5 red marbles and 2 blue marbles in a bag. Draw the marbles. Color them. Which color marble is she more likely to pick?

_____

Draw here.

Use with text pages 253–255.

Count Tens

You can count crayons by ones.

You can also make groups of ten.

10 ones equal 1 ten.

Use ⬭ .

Write the number of tens shown. Then write the number.

1.

_____3____ tens

_____30___ thirty

2.

_____ tens

_____ fifty

3.

_____ tens

_____ forty

Make groups of ten. Draw the tens.

Write the number.

4. 2 tens

_____ twenty

Use with text pages 277–278.

Teen Numbers

Making groups of ten can help you count.

Workmat 3

Tens	Ones

12 ones

Regroup 12 ones as 1 ten and 2 ones.

Workmat 3

Tens	Ones

_1_ ten _2_ ones

Use small items such as dried beans or pasta.
Regroup. Write the tens and the ones.
Then write the number.

1. 18 ones _____ ten _____ ones _____

2. 12 ones _____ ten _____ ones _____

3. 15 ones _____ ten _____ ones _____

4. Draw 13 of your favorite stickers in the box. How many groups of ten are there? How many ones are there?

_____ ten _____ ones

Use with text pages 279–280.

Name _____ Date _____

Tens and Ones

Making groups of ten can help you count.

Workmat 3

Tens	Ones

22 ones

Regroup **22** ones as **2** tens and **2** ones.

Workmat 3

Tens	Ones

_2_ ten _2_ ones

Use small items such as coins or macaroni.
Regroup. Write the tens and the ones.

Then write the number.

1. 14 ones   _1_ ten _4_ ones   _14_

2. 23 ones   _____ tens _____ ones   _____

3. 31 ones   _____ tens _____ one   _____

4. Draw 25 marbles in the jar.
   Circle the groups of ten. How
   many groups of ten are there?
   How many ones are there?

   _____ tens _____ ones

Use with text pages 281–282.

Numbers Through 50

You can show a number as
tens and ones.

Tens	Ones
⌇⌇⌇⌇ ⌇⌇⌇⌇	▯▯▯

__2__ tens __3__ ones __23__
twenty-three

Use small items such as buttons or coins.

Show the tens and ones.

Write the tens and the ones. Then write the number.

1.

Tens	Ones
⌇⌇⌇⌇ ⌇⌇⌇⌇ ⌇⌇⌇⌇	▯▯▯▯

_____ tens _____ ones _____
thirty-four

2.

Tens	Ones
⌇⌇⌇⌇ ⌇⌇⌇⌇	▯▯▯▯▯ ▯▯

_____ tens _____ ones _____
twenty-seven

3. Use paper clips. Show a number to a family
   member. Include at least one group of ten.
   Have the family member say the number you
   are showing. Take turns showing and telling.

Use with text pages 283–284.

Numbers Through 99

You can use tens and ones to show numbers to 99. Here are ways to show 74.

Tens	Ones

_74_
seventy-four

Write the tens and the ones. Then write the number.

1.

Tens	Ones

Tens	Ones

_____
twenty-six

2.

Tens	Ones

Tens	Ones

_____
fourty-four

3.

Tens	Ones

Tens	Ones

_____
thirty-five

4.

Tens	Ones

Tens	Ones

_____
ninety-two

5. Marla has six boxes of crayons. Each box holds 10 crayons. Lois gives her 3 more crayons. Write the number of crayons Marla has now.

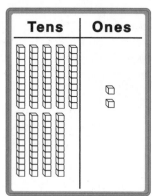

Tens	Ones

_____
sixty-three

Use with text pages 285–287.

Place Value Through 99

Rita looks at the cubes.

She writes 9 in the tens place.

She writes 3 in the ones place.

Then she writes the number.

Tens	Ones
9	3

93

ninety-three

Write the tens in the tens place.
Write the ones in the ones place.
Then write the number.

1.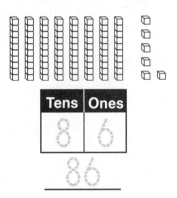

Tens	Ones
8	6

86

2.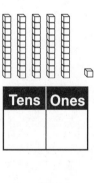

Tens	Ones

_____

3.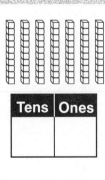

Tens	Ones

_____

4.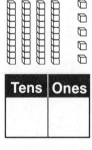

Tens	Ones

_____

5. Manuel has 8 boxes of crayons. Each box has 10 crayons. Ruth gives him 3 more crayons. Write how many crayons he has now.

Tens	Ones

_____ crayons

Use with text pages 289–290.

Name _____ Date _____

Different Ways to Show Numbers

You can write a number in different ways.

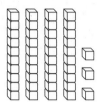

___4__ tens ___3__ ones

__40__ + __3__ = __43__

Write each number in different ways.

1.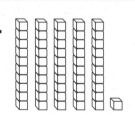

_____ tens _____ ones

_____ + _____ = _____

2.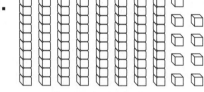

_____ tens _____ ones

_____ + _____ = _____

3.

_____ tens _____ one

_____ + _____ = _____

4. Work with a family member to show numbers with beans. Take turns writing and saying the number in different ways.

Write here.

Use with text pages 291–292.

Numbers Through 100

When you count by ones, the number after 99 is 100.

10 tens = 100   100   one hundred

Write how many tens and ones. Write the number.

1. ___8___ tens ___2___ ones

___82___

eighty-two

2. _____ tens _____ ones

_____

twenty-nine

3. _____ tens _____ ones

_____

ninety-nine

4. 10 friends pick up cans at the beach. Each friend picks up 10 cans. How many cans do they have in all?

_____ cans

Draw or write to explain.

Use with text pages 293–294.

Name _____ Date _____

Problem Solving:
Act It Out With Models

You can use small objects such as buttons to act out the problem.

Alita has 23 tulips.

She wants to plant rows of 10 tulips in each row.

How many rows does Alita need?

Alita will need 3 rows.

Solve.

Draw or write to explain.

1. Nan puts 68 seashells in boxes.
   Each box holds 10 shells.
   How many boxes does Nan need?   _____ boxes

2. Zac has 43 books. He puts
   10 books on each shelf. How
   many shelves does he need?   _____ shelves

Use with text pages 295–297.

Name _____ Date _____

Order Numbers

Look at the number line.

```
←—+——+——+——+——+——+——+——(+)——+——+——+—→
  90  91  92  93  94  95  96 (97) 98  99 100
```

96 comes before 97.

98 comes after 97.

Use the number line.

Write the number that comes before, after, or between.

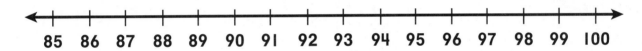

```
←—+——+——+——+——+——+——+——+——+——+——+——+——+——+——+——+—→
  85  86  87  88  89  90  91  92  93  94  95  96  97  98  99 100
```

1. 89, __90__

2. ____, 87

3. 92, ____

4. ____, 100

5. 93, ____, 95

6. 85, ____, 87

7. Ben has to pick a number for his baseball shirt. He wants the number just after 14. What number does Ben want?

____

Use with text pages 305–306.

Ordinal Numbers

Some words tell the position of someone or something.

first   second   third   fourth   fifth

Color.

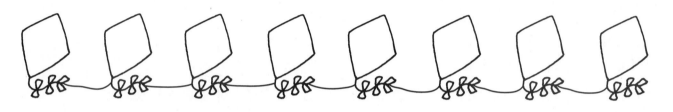

1. first

⬜ Red ⬜

2. fourth

⬜ Green ⬜

3. eighth

⬜ Yellow ⬜

4. sixth

⬜ Blue ⬜

5. second

⬜ Black ⬜

6. seventh

⬜ Brown ⬜

7. Eli is second in line for lunch.
Meg is right behind him. What
position in line does Meg have?

_____

Use with text pages 307–308.

Name ____________________ Date ________

Homework 11.3

Use Ten to Estimate

When you do not need to know the exact number, you can estimate.

Circle one group of ten.
Estimate how many in all. Then count.

1. 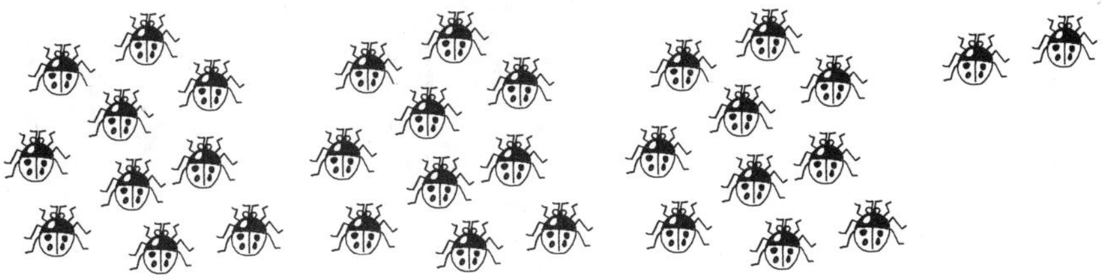

Estimate 30

Count 32

2. 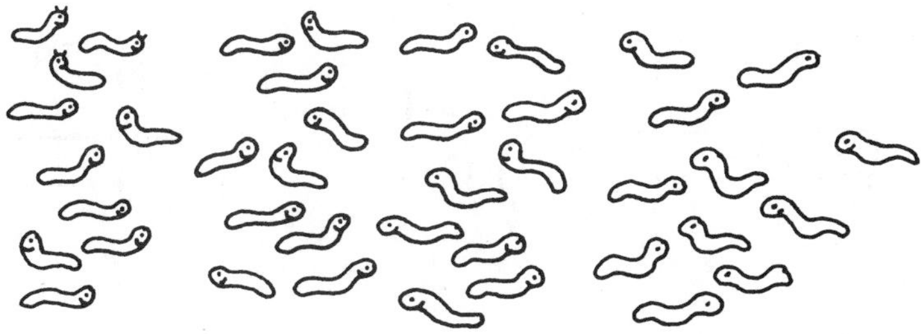

Estimate ______

Count ______

3. 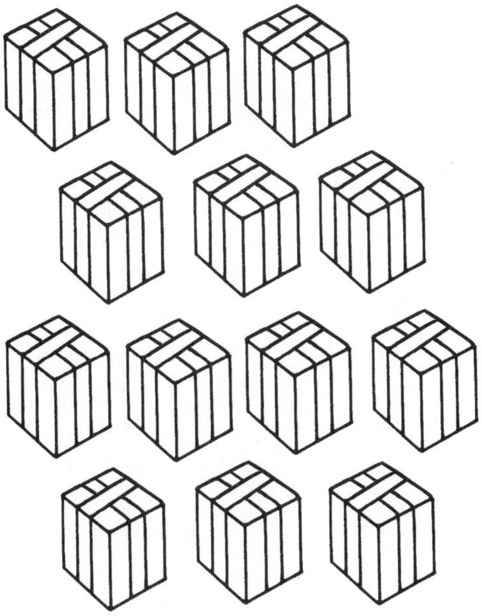

Eva wants to buy enough bows to put one on each friend's party gift. She knows she can estimate to get an idea of how many. Estimate with Eva. Then count the boxes with her. How many did you estimate? How many did you count?

Estimate ______

Count ______

Use with text pages 309–311.

Name _____ Date _____

Greater Than, Less Than

You can compare numbers using the words **greater than** and **less than**.

Circle the number that is greater.

1.

2.

Circle the number that is less.

3.

4.

5. Matt likes to play a thinking game with his friend Melvin. Matt says, I am thinking of a number that is greater than **6** but less than **8**. What number am I thinking of? Melvin knows the right answer. What number will Melvin say?

The number is _____.

Use with text pages 313–314.

Name _____ Date _____

Use Symbols to Compare Numbers

> means greater than.
    20 > 10
< means less than.
    5 < 10
= means is equal to.
    5 = 5

Compare the numbers. Circle >, <, or =.

1.    >
        <
        =

2.    >
        <
        =

3.    >
        <
        =

4. Keri sees this sign.

| The number of beans > 75. |
| The number of beans < 85. |

Use the clues to make a guess
about how many beans may
be in the jar. Circle.

60 beans   82 beans   90 beans

Use with text pages 315–316.

Problem Solving:
Reasonable Answers

About how many books will fit in
Ellie's backpack?

about 50   ⟨ about 5 ⟩

5 books is the answer. It makes more sense.

Estimate. Circle the answer
that makes more sense.

1. About how many hours did
Linda spend at the library
today?

about 2 hours

about 20 hours

2. About how many coins
can Nicki hold in one hand?

about 100 coins

about 10 coins

3. About how many muffins
can Sheila eat at one
meal?

about 16

about 2

4. About how many kittens
can fit in a small basket?

about 4

about 24

Use with text pages 317–318.

Count by Twos

What number comes next if you skip count by 2s?

56, 58, __60__

1	2	3	4	5	6	7	8	9	10
11	12	13	14	15	16	17	18	19	20
21	22	23	24	25	26	27	28	29	30
31	32	33	34	35	36	37	38	39	40
41	42	43	44	45	46	47	48	49	50
51	52	53	54	55	56	57	58	59	60
61	62	63	64	65	66	67	68	69	70
71	72	73	74	75	76	77	78	79	80
81	82	83	84	85	86	87	88	89	90
91	92	93	94	95	96	97	98	99	100

Write the missing numbers. Skip count by 2s.

1. 8, __10__, 12, __14__

2. _____, 54, _____, 58

3. 18, _____, _____, 24

4. 80, _____, 84, _____

5. 32, _____, 36, _____

6. _____, 46, _____, 50

7. 76, _____, _____, 82

8. 88, _____, 92, _____

9. Find things in your home to skip count by 2s. For example, you might count shoes in your closet. The first pair is 2 shoes, the next pair is 4 shoes, and so on. Write how you counted the items.

Draw or write here.

Use with text pages 325–326.

Count by Fives

What number comes next
if you skip count by 5s?

1	2	3	4	5	6	7	8	9	10
11	12	13	14	15	16	17	18	19	20
21	22	23	24	25	26	27	28	29	30
31	32	33	34	35	36	37	38	39	40
41	42	43	44	45	46	47	48	49	50
51	52	53	54	55	56	57	58	59	60
61	62	63	64	65	66	67	68	69	70
71	72	73	74	75	76	77	78	79	80
81	82	83	84	85	86	87	88	89	90
91	92	93	94	95	96	97	98	99	100

65, 70, __75__
The number 75 comes next.

Write the missing numbers.
Skip count by 5s.

1. 5, __10__, 15, __20__

2. ____, 55, ____, 65

3. 65, ____, ____, 80

4. 85, ____, 95, ____

5. 30, ____, 40, ____

6. ____, 75, ____, 85

7. 20, ____, ____, 35

8. 15, ____, 25, ____

9. Marci puts 5 stickers on each page. She skip counts by 5s to see how many stickers she has. Think of things you can skip count by 5s. Count them.

Draw or write here.

Use with text pages 327–328.

More Than, Less Than

You can use the words more than and less than
when you talk about number patterns.

Use this table to write
the numbers.

1	2	3	4	5	6	7	8	9	10
11	12	13	14	15	16	17	18	19	20
21	22	23	24	25	26	27	28	29	30
31	32	33	34	35	36	37	38	39	40
41	42	43	44	45	46	47	48	49	50
51	52	53	54	55	56	57	58	59	60
61	62	63	64	65	66	67	68	69	70
71	72	73	74	75	76	77	78	79	80
81	82	83	84	85	86	87	88	89	90
91	92	93	94	95	96	97	98	99	100

1. This number is 1 more.

28 __29__

2. This number is 1 less.

_____ 19

3. This number is 10 more.

15 _____

4. This number is 10 less.

_____ 22

5. How old are you? _____

You were 1 less year last
year. How old were you
then? _____

How old will you be in
10 more years? _____

Draw or write here.

Use with text pages 329–330.

Name _____ Date _____

Even and Odd Numbers

You can make pairs with an
even number of shoes.
8 is an even number.

If you have pairs with one left
over, you have an odd number.
9 is an odd number.

even   odd

Circle even or odd.

1.

odd

even

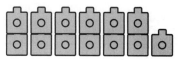

2.

odd

even

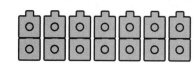

3.

odd

even

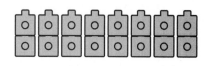

4.

odd

even

5. How many children live in
your building or on your
block or road? How would
you line them up? Is there
an even number of children
or an odd number?

Draw or write here.

Use with text pages 333–334.

Problem Solving:
Find a Pattern

Dino does 2 pages of homework on Monday.

He does 2 more pages each day through Friday.

How many pages of homework does Dino do in one week?

Understand

What do I know?

I know that Dino does 2 pages of homework
each day of the school week.

Plan

I can use a pattern to solve.

I'll circle the strategy I will use.

Draw a picture.
Make a table.
Use models.

M	T	W	Th	F
2				

Solve Find the pattern.

I can make a table with the
days of the week on top.

I begin with 2 pages the first day.
I can skip count by 2s to fill in
the other numbers.

Dino does _____ pages of homework a week.

Look Back

Did I answer the question?
Does my answer make sense?

Use with text pages 335–337.

Name _____ Date _____

Order Events

Events happen in an order.
This is what happens when you feed a cat.

Some events happen before.

Some events happen after.

1. Write 1, 2, and 3 to show the correct order.

_____   _____   _____

2. Think about what happens
   when you put on a sock.
   Draw a picture to show
   what you do before.
   Draw a picture to show
   what you do after.

Draw here.

Use with text pages 359–360.

Name _____ Date _____

Activity: Estimate a Minute

You can read a page in about I minute.

It takes more than I minute to read a book.

You can read a sign in less than I minute.

Use a clock to time I minute.

Circle the activity if it takes about I minute.

Draw an X on the activity if it takes more than I minute.

I. Take a bath. 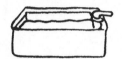	**2.** Write the alphabet. 
3. Open a gift. 	**4.** Open a door.
5. Eat breakfast. 	**6.** Write your name.

7. Think of two activities that take more than I minute and two that take less than I minute. Act them out to see if you are right.

Use with text pages 361–362.

Hour

Some clocks show the time with a minute hand and an hour hand.

I o'clock

Other clocks show the time using only numbers.

I o'clock

`1:00`

Draw a line to match clocks that tell the same time.

1.

`4:00`

2.

`8:00`

3.

`2:00`

4. Think of an hour in the day that is important to you. Draw a clock with hands and show the time. Draw a clock that uses only numbers. Show the time of day on that clock.

Draw here.

Use with text pages 363–364.

Name _____ Date _____

Half-Hour

An hour is
60 minutes.

3:00
3 o'clock

A half-hour is
30 minutes.

3:30
half past **3**

Say and write the time.

1.

half past _____

2.

_____ o'clock

3.

half past _____

4.

_____ o'clock

5. Write down **3** activities you do each day. Think about the hour or half-hour you usually do each activity. Write the time of each activity.

Write here.

Use with text pages 365–367.

Elapsed Time

The minute hand goes around the clock
one time to show 1 hour has passed.

 The clock says 6 o'clock.

 The clock says 7 o'clock.
6 to 7 is the same as 6 + 1 = 7.
6 o'clock to 7 o'clock is 1 hour.

Draw the clock hands to show when the activity ended.

1. It takes 1 hour
   to cook dinner.

2. It takes 2 hours
   to watch a movie.

3. On the clocks, show the
   hour or half-hour when you
   get up in the morning and
   when you go to bed at
   night. How many hours will
   you be awake today?

_____ hours awake

Use with text pages 369–371.

Practice Telling Time

The same time can be shown on different clocks.

You can use a clock with hands to tell time.

You can use a digital clock to tell time.

2:30

Show the time on the two clocks.

1. half past 9

2. 6 o' clock

3. half past 4

 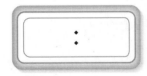

4. Count the number of clocks in your home. How many have hands? How many are digital?

Draw or write here.

Use with text pages 373–374.

Name _____ Date _____

Days and Weeks

Fill in the calendar for next month.

Sunday	Monday	Tuesday	Wednesday	Thursday	Friday	Saturday

Answer the questions.

1. What is the name of the month? _____

2. On what day of the week
   does the month begin? _____

3. On what day of the week
   does the month end? _____

4. How many days are in this month? _____

5. Count the number of days
   you will go to school. Count
   the vacation days. Count
   the weekend days.

   There are _____ days of school
   this month.

   There are _____ vacation days.

   There are _____ weekend days.

Use with text pages 375–376.

Months

There are 12 months in one year. They are:

January, February, March, April, May, June, July, August, September, October, November, December.

Use the calendars to answer the questions.

1. Which month comes before May?

April

2. Which month has the most days?

_____

3. Which month has 5 Wednesdays?

_____

4. Finish this sentence. 30 days has September, _____, _____, and November.

5. In which month is your birthday? Write the month. Write the months that come before and after.

April

Sun.	Mon.	Tues.	Wed.	Thurs.	Fri.	Sat.
		1	2	3	4	5
6	7	8	9	10	11	12
13	14	15	16	17	18	19
20	21	22	23	24	25	26
27	28	29	30			

May

Sun.	Mon.	Tues.	Wed.	Thurs.	Fri.	Sat.
				1	2	3
4	5	6	7	8	9	10
11	12	13	14	15	16	17
18	19	20	21	22	23	24
25	26	27	28	29	30	31

June

Sun.	Mon.	Tues.	Wed.	Thurs.	Fri.	Sat.
1	2	3	4	5	6	7
8	9	10	11	12	13	14
15	16	17	18	19	20	21
22	23	24	25	26	27	28
29	30					

Write here.

Use with text pages 377–378.

Name _____ Date _____

Problem Solving: Use a Table

You can organize information in a table.

If Lila played outside for an hour, when would she begin dinner?

Activity	Lila's Time	My Time
Play outside	5:00	
Dinner	6:00	
Homework	7:00	
Bath	8:00	

Use the table to solve.

Lila plays outside

at _____ o'clock.

A half-hour later it is _____ .

Lila could begin dinner at _____ .

Now fill in the table with the time you begin each activity.

1. How long do you do your homework?

   I do homework for _____ minutes.

2. How many hours is it from the time you begin dinner until the time you take a bath?

   It is _____ hours from the time I begin dinner until the time I take a bath.

3. What activity takes the most amount of time?

   _____ is the longest activity of my evening.

Use with text pages 379–381.

Value of Coins

You can count on to find the value of the coins.

Count pennies by ones.

_1_ ¢ _2_ ¢ _3_ ¢

Count nickels by fives.

_5_ ¢ _10_ ¢ _15_ ¢

Count dimes by tens.

_10_ ¢ _20_ ¢ _30_ ¢

Count on by ones, fives, or tens.
Write the final amount.

1.

___ ¢ ___ ¢ ___ ¢ ___ ¢ ___ ¢   ___ ¢

2.

___ ¢ ___ ¢ ___ ¢ ___ ¢ ___ ¢   ___ ¢

3.

___ ¢ ___ ¢ ___ ¢ ___ ¢   ___ ¢

4. Think of two ways to make **30¢** with coins. Draw two ways on the back of this paper.

Use with text pages 389–390.

Nickels and Pennies

To find the value of the coins,
count the coin with the greater value first.

_5_ ¢ _10_ ¢ _____ ¢ _____ ¢ _____ ¢

Count on by fives
for nickels.
Count on by ones
for pennies.

What is the value of each group of coins?
Use coins to help solve.

		How much?
1.	_____ ¢ _____ ¢ _____ ¢ _____ ¢ _____ ¢	_____ ¢
2.	_____ ¢ _____ ¢ _____ ¢ _____ ¢ _____ ¢ _____ ¢	_____ ¢
3.	_____ ¢ _____ ¢ _____ ¢ _____ ¢ _____ ¢ _____ ¢	_____ ¢

4. You can trade 5 pennies for 1 nickel.
Fill out the chart to show how many
pennies or nickels you need to trade.

Is there a pattern in the chart? _____

What is it? _____

pennies	nickels
5	1
10	
	3
	4
25	

Use with text pages 391–392.

Name _____ Date _____

Dimes and Pennies

To find the value of the coins,
count the coin with the greater value first.

Count on by tens for dimes.

Count on by ones for pennies.

_10_ ¢ _20_ ¢ ____ ¢ ____ ¢ ____ ¢ ____ ¢

Circle the coins that match the number of cents shown.
Use coins to help you solve.

1. 22¢	
2. 30¢	
3. 15¢	

4. How many dimes and
   pennies would you need
   to make 53¢?

Draw or write to explain.

____ dimes ____ pennies

Use with text pages 393–394.

Count Coins

You can find the value of coins by counting on.

Count dimes first.

10¢ __20__ ¢

Count nickels next.

25¢ __30__ ¢ __35__ ¢

Then count pennies.

36¢   37¢ __38__ ¢ __39__ ¢

39¢

Find the value of the coins. Use dimes, nickels, and pennies.

1.

____ ¢ ____ ¢ ____ ¢ ____ ¢ ____ ¢   ____ ¢

2.

____ ¢ ____ ¢ ____ ¢ ____ ¢ ____ ¢   ____ ¢

3. Carla has 3 dimes, 3 nickels, and 4 pennies. Can she buy an apple that costs 49¢? Circle Yes or No.

Yes   No

Draw or write to explain.

Use with text pages 395–396.

Quarters

A quarter is equal to **25¢**.
Circle the coins that make **25¢**.

1.

2.

Circle the coins that match the price.

3.  **54¢**	 
4. **42¢**	

5. Show **18¢** with fewer coins.

Draw or write to explain.

Use with text pages 399–401.

Dollar

A set of coins with a value of 100 cents equals one dollar.
You can skip count to find the value of the coins.

__25__ ¢ __50__ ¢ __75__ ¢ __80__ ¢ __85__ ¢ __90__ ¢ __100__ ¢ $ __1__

Find the value of the coins.

1.

_____ ¢ _____ ¢ _____ ¢ _____ ¢ _____ ¢ _____ ¢

_____ ¢ _____ ¢ _____ ¢ _____ ¢ _____ ¢ $ ____

2.

_____ ¢ _____ ¢ _____ ¢ _____ ¢ _____ ¢ _____ ¢ $ ____

3. Gina has only nickels in her piggy bank. How can she
make a dollar?

Use with text pages 403–404.

Name _____ Date _____

Problem Solving: Use a Picture

The school fair had three booths with food.

Use the picture to help you decide how much money is needed.

1. Sam wants to buy lemonade and popcorn. He has 21¢. What other coins does he need?

_____

2. Cindy uses her money to buy apples for her friends. She has a dime and four nickels. How many apples can she buy?

_____ apples

Use coins and the picture to solve.

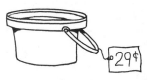  

3. Sue wants to use dimes to buy the beach ball. How many dimes does she need?

_____ dimes

4. Hans has 2 dimes, 1 nickel, and 4 pennies. What item can he buy?

_____

Use with text pages 405–407.

Count On to Add

Find $3 + 6$.
Start with the greater number, 6.
Count on 3 to find the sum.

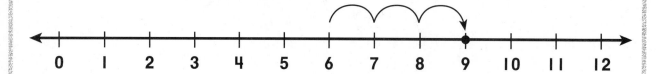

$$3 + 6 = 9$$

Use the number line. Write the sum.

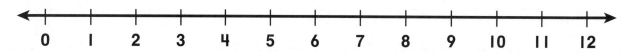

1. $\begin{array}{r} 5 \\ + 3 \\ \hline 8 \end{array}$

2. $\begin{array}{r} 2 \\ + 8 \\ \hline \end{array}$

3. $\begin{array}{r} 7 \\ + 3 \\ \hline \end{array}$

4. $\begin{array}{r} 6 \\ + 2 \\ \hline \end{array}$

5. $10 + 2 =$ _____

6. $7 + 2 =$ _____

7. $4 + 1 =$ _____

8. $9 + 3 =$ _____

9. Maia and Tina find shells on the beach. Maia finds 6 shells. Tina finds 3 shells. How many shells did the girls find in all?

    _____ shells in all

Draw or write.

Use with text pages 429–430.

Sums of 10

There are different ways to make the sum of 10.

$6 + 4 = 10$ $5 + 5 = 10$ $2 + 8 = 10$

Count the circles. Fill in blanks with circles to make 10.

Write an addition sentence for each row.

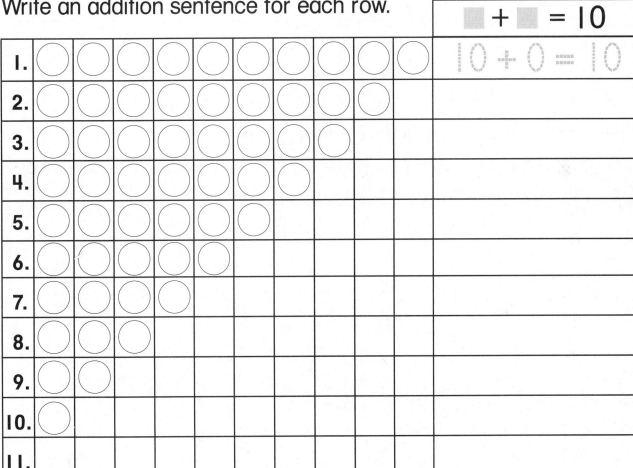

											$\blacksquare + \blacksquare = 10$
1.	○	○	○	○	○	○	○	○	○	○	10 + 0 = 10
2.	○	○	○	○	○	○	○	○	○		
3.	○	○	○	○	○	○	○				
4.	○	○	○	○	○	○					
5.	○	○	○	○	○						
6.	○	○	○	○							
7.	○	○	○								
8.	○	○									
9.	○	○									
10.	○										
11.											

12. Tan needs to set the table for
10 people in all. He has already
placed 6 plates on the table. How
many more plates must he place
to get the sum of 10 plates in all?

Draw or write to explain.

$6 + \underline{\quad} = 10$

Use with text pages 431–432.

Name _____ Date _____

Making 10 to Add

Use making 10 to find sums greater than 10.

Julio wants 12 pieces of macaroni.
He already has 7 pieces.
How many pieces of macaroni
does he add to make 12? _____

$$7 + 5 = 12$$

Use small objects to match the number of things
you see. Then put down more to complete the addition sentence.
Write the missing number in the addition sentence.

1. ___10___ + _____ = 11

2. ___5___ + _____ = 12

3. ___9___ + _____ = 11

4. ___3___ + _____ = 11

5. Kyla will win a prize if she can pick 2 numbers from a box that will add up to 11. What are 2 numbers Kyla could pick to win the prize?

Draw or write.

Use with text pages 433–434.

Order Property

You can add numbers in any order
and get the same sum.

$$3 + 5 = 8 \qquad 5 + 3 = 8$$

Complete the chart.

1.	3 + ____	9 + ____	12
2.	1 + ____	8 + ____	9
3.	4 + ____	7 + ____	11

Find the sums.

4.   6   5   5.   2   6   6.   7   3

     + 5   + 6   + 6   + 2   + 3   + 7

7. Mica wants to pack 12 apples in a box. So far, he has put 9 apples in the box. How many more should he put in to get 12 apples in all?

Draw or write to explain.

____ apples

Use with text pages 435–436.

Name _____ Date _____

Addition Facts Practice

You can use different strategies to find sums.

Count on 6 + 2 = 8   Say 6. Count 7, 8.

Use doubles 3 + 3 = 6   The addends are the same.

Use doubles plus one 5 + 6 = 11   5 + 5 and 1 more.

Make ten 3 + 7 = 10

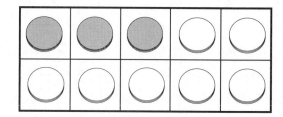

Find the sum.

1. 2 + 3 = 5

2. 6 + 3 = ____

3. 3 + 4 = ____

4. 5 + 3 = ____

5. 4 + 4 = ____

6. 4 + 6 = ____

7. 5
   + 3
   ____

8. 8
   + 4
   ____

9. 6
   + 6
   ____

10. Cindy has 5 marbles. She buys 4 more marbles. How many marbles does she have in all? Tell what strategy you used to find the sum.

____ marbles

Draw or write to explain.

Use with text pages 439–442.

Add Three Numbers

You can add three numbers in any order. First, find the sum of two numbers. Then, add the third number.

$$
\begin{array}{r} 5 \\ 3 \\ +4 \end{array} \quad
\begin{array}{r} \boxed{8} \\ +4 \\ \hline 12 \end{array} \quad \text{or} \quad
\begin{array}{r} 5 \\ 3 \\ +4 \end{array} \; \boxed{7} \;
\begin{array}{r} +5 \\ \hline 12 \end{array} \quad \text{or} \quad
\begin{array}{r} 5 \\ 3 \\ +4 \end{array} \;
\begin{array}{r} 3 \\ +\boxed{9} \\ \hline 12 \end{array}
$$

Write the sum.

1.
$$\begin{array}{r} 6 \\ 3 \\ +3 \\ \hline 12 \end{array}$$

2.
$$\begin{array}{r} 4 \\ 5 \\ +2 \\ \hline \end{array}$$

3.
$$\begin{array}{r} 1 \\ 4 \\ +5 \\ \hline \end{array}$$

4.
$$\begin{array}{r} 4 \\ 1 \\ +2 \\ \hline \end{array}$$

5.
$$\begin{array}{r} 8 \\ 1 \\ +3 \\ \hline \end{array}$$

6.
$$\begin{array}{r} 4 \\ 2 \\ +3 \\ \hline \end{array}$$

7.
$$\begin{array}{r} 2 \\ 8 \\ +2 \\ \hline \end{array}$$

8.
$$\begin{array}{r} 6 \\ 1 \\ +3 \\ \hline \end{array}$$

9. Alice has to find the sum of 3, 5, and 3. She adds 3 + 3 first. Tell why. _____

_____

_____

$$\begin{array}{r} 3 \\ 5 \\ +3 \\ \hline \end{array}$$

Use with text pages 443–444.

Name _____ Date _____

Missing Addends

Sometimes you know one addend and the sum. Find the missing addend.

$4 + \underline{} = 7$

Use objects.
Find the missing addend.

1.

$6 + \underline{6} = 12$

2.

$7 + \underline{} = 9$

3.

$\underline{} + 5 = 12$

4.

$\underline{} + 5 = 11$

5.

$\underline{} + 3 = 8$

6.

$\underline{} + 4 = 11$

7. Beth needs 6 hats for her party. She already has 3. Find the missing addend.

$3 + \underline{} = 6$

Draw or write to explain.

Use with text pages 445–446.

Problem Solving: Make a Table

You can make a table to solve problems.
Complete the table and solve.

1.

Kind of Sandwich	Number
Cheese	4
Peanut butter	7
Turkey	2

2. How many turkey sandwiches are there?

_____

3. How many peanut butter sandwiches and cheese sandwiches are there?

_____

4. How many more cheese sandwiches than turkey are there?

_____

5. Jerry eats 2 peanut butter sandwiches for lunch. Elise makes 1 peanut butter sandwich and adds it to the plate. How many peanut butter sandwiches are there now?

_____

Use with text pages 447–449.

Count Back to Subtract

Count back on a number line to subtract.

Find $9 - 3$.

Start from 9. Count back 3.

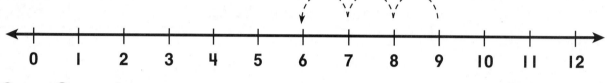

$9 - 3 = 6$

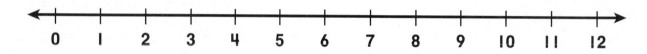

Use the number line. Subtract.

1. $8 - 3 = \underline{5}$

2. $10 - 2 = \underline{}$

3. $12 - 2 = \underline{}$

4. $11 - 1 = \underline{}$

5. $\begin{array}{r} 6 \\ -3 \\ \hline \end{array}$

6. $\begin{array}{r} 11 \\ -3 \\ \hline \end{array}$

7. $\begin{array}{r} 7 \\ -2 \\ \hline \end{array}$

8. $\begin{array}{r} 10 \\ -1 \\ \hline \end{array}$

9. Put 12 buttons on a table. Take 3 away. How many are left?

_____ buttons

Draw or explain here.

Use with text pages 457–458.

Parts and Wholes

If you know the whole and one of the parts, you can find the other part.

$$11 - 4 = \underline{7}$$
$$11 - 7 = 4$$

Whole	
11	
Part	Part
4	?

Write the difference.

Whole	
12	
Red	Yellow
10	?

Whole	
10	
Red	Yellow
?	4

1. $12 - 10 = \underline{2}$

   $12 - \ 2 = \underline{\hspace{1cm}}$

2. $10 - 4 = \underline{\hspace{1cm}}$

   $10 - 6 = \underline{\hspace{1cm}}$

3.
$$\begin{array}{r} 9 \\ -3 \\ \hline \end{array} \qquad \begin{array}{r} 9 \\ -6 \\ \hline \end{array}$$

4.
$$\begin{array}{r} 11 \\ -5 \\ \hline \end{array} \qquad \begin{array}{r} 11 \\ -6 \\ \hline \end{array}$$

5. Place 11 buttons on a table. Look away. Have a family member take away buttons. Look back. How many buttons are left? How many buttons were taken away?

_____ buttons left

_____ buttons taken

Use with text pages 459–460.

Name _____ Date _____

Relate Addition and Subtraction

An addition fact and a subtraction fact that
have the same numbers are related facts.

$$6 + 5 = 11$$
$$11 - 5 = 6$$

Use related facts to add and subtract.

1. $\begin{array}{r} 4 \\ + 6 \\ \hline 10 \end{array}$ $\begin{array}{r} 10 \\ - 6 \\ \hline 4 \end{array}$

2. $\begin{array}{r} 8 \\ + 3 \\ \hline \end{array}$ $\begin{array}{r} 11 \\ - 3 \\ \hline \end{array}$

3. $\begin{array}{r} 7 \\ + 5 \\ \hline \end{array}$ $\begin{array}{r} 12 \\ - 5 \\ \hline \end{array}$

4. $\begin{array}{r} 1 \\ + 8 \\ \hline \end{array}$ $\begin{array}{r} 9 \\ - 8 \\ \hline \end{array}$

5. $\begin{array}{r} 7 \\ + 3 \\ \hline \end{array}$ $\begin{array}{r} 10 \\ - 3 \\ \hline \end{array}$

6. $\begin{array}{r} 3 \\ + 9 \\ \hline \end{array}$ $\begin{array}{r} 12 \\ - 9 \\ \hline \end{array}$

7. Jennifer has 6 rings.
   She gets 2 more for her
   birthday. How many rings
   does she have in all?

   _____ rings

8. Then Jennifer gives 2
   rings to her sister. How
   many rings does she have
   left?

   _____ rings

Use with text pages 461–462.

Subtraction Facts Practice

You can use different strategies to find differences.

Count back. $10 - 7 = 3$ Say 10. Count 9, 8, 7.

Use parts and wholes.

Whole
8

Part	Part
3	?

$8 - 3 = 5$

$8 - 5 = 3$

Relate addition and subtraction. $7 + 5 = 12,\ 12 - 5 = 7$

Find the difference.

1. $6 - 4 = $ _____

2. $11 - 7 = $ _____

3. $9 - 2 = $ _____

4. $12 - 9 = $ _____

5. $8 - 4 = $ _____

6. $10 - 7 = $ _____

7.
$$\begin{array}{r} 12 \\ -10 \\ \hline \end{array}$$

8.
$$\begin{array}{r} 7 \\ -2 \\ \hline \end{array}$$

9.
$$\begin{array}{r} 9 \\ -5 \\ \hline \end{array}$$

10. Katie sees 11 parakeets at the pet store. 6 are blue. The rest are yellow. How many yellow parakeets are at the pet store? Tell what strategy you used to find the difference.

_____ yellow parakeets

Draw or write to explain.

Use with text pages 465–468.

Fact Families for 11

A fact family has the same numbers.

This fact family has the numbers
11, 6, and 5.

Whole	
11	
Red	Yellow
6	5

$6 + 5 =$ _____ $11 - 6 =$ _____

$5 + 6 =$ _____ $11 - 5 =$ _____

Complete the fact family.

1.

11	
4	7

$4 + 7 =$ _11_ $11 - 4 =$ _7_

$7 + 4 =$ _11_ $11 - 7 =$ _4_

2.

11	
2	9

$2 + 9 =$ _____ $11 - 2 =$ _____

$9 + 2 =$ _____ $11 - 9 =$ _____

3.

11	
8	3

$8 + 3 =$ _____ $11 - 3 =$ _____

$3 + 8 =$ _____ $11 - 8 =$ _____

4. The price tag on a bottle of juice is 9¢. You have 6¢ and your friend has 3¢. Complete the fact family for these numbers.

_____ + _____ = _____

_____ + _____ = _____

_____ − _____ = _____

_____ − _____ = _____

Use with text pages 469–470.

Fact Families for 12

A fact family is a group of facts
that share the same numbers.

The facts in a fact family are related.
The numbers 12, 8, and 4 make a fact family.

Whole	
12	
Red	**Yellow**
4	8

$$4 + 8 = 12 \qquad 12 - 4 = 8$$
$$8 + 4 = 12 \qquad 12 - 8 = 4$$

Complete the fact family.

1.

12	
5	7

$5 + 7 = \underline{12}$ $12 - 5 = \underline{}$

$7 + 5 = \underline{}$ $\underline{}\bigcirc\underline{} = \underline{}$

2.

12	
6	6

$6 + 6 = \underline{}$ $\underline{}\bigcirc\underline{}\bigcirc\underline{}$

3.

12	
3	9

$3 + 9 = \underline{}$ $12 - 3 = \underline{}$

$9 + 3 = \underline{}$ $\underline{}\bigcirc\underline{} = \underline{}$

4. Write a fact family for
these flowers.

$\underline{} + \underline{} = \underline{}$

$\underline{} + \underline{} = \underline{}$

$\underline{} - \underline{} = \underline{}$

$\underline{} - \underline{} = \underline{}$

Use with text pages 471–472.

Names for Numbers

8	(2 + 6)	5 + 7	10 − 4	(9 − 1)
	5 + 4	(4 + 4)	(11 − 3)	8 + 2

Circle the names for the number.

1.

6	3 + 3	4 − 2	1 + 2 + 3
	2 + 4	(5 + 1)	3 + 3 + 1

2.

7	9 − 2	4 − 3	1 + 2 + 4
	5 − 2	7 − 0	5 + 2

3.

10	5 − 5	12 − 2	5 + 5 + 0
	6 − 4	1 + 9	3 + 3 + 4

4. Leo has 6 marbles. Write three
different names for the number
of marbles.

Write here.

Use with text pages 473–474.

Problem Solving:
Choose the Operation

You can use addition or subtraction to solve a problem.

There are **6** guinea pigs in a cage.

Gail buys **2** of them.

How many guinea pigs are left?

UNDERSTAND

What do I need to find out?   I need to find out how many guinea pigs are _____.

What do I know?   I know there are _____ guinea pigs and Gail buys _____ of them.

PLAN

What operation do I use?   _____

SOLVE

What number sentence can I write to solve the problem?   _____ ◯ _____ ◯ _____

LOOK BACK

Is there another way I could solve the problem?

Use with text pages 475–477.

Name _____ Date _____

Activity: Compare and Order Length

Use taller and shorter when you compare height.

Use longer and shorter when you compare length.

Taller   Shorter

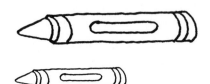

Longer

Shorter

Compare and order length and height.

1. Color the shorter crayon green.
   Color the longer crayon red.

2. Draw a crayon that is longer than the red crayon.

Draw here.

3. Find a tablespoon, a fork, and a teaspoon. Order them from shortest to longest. Find other objects to compare.

Write your results here.

Use with text pages 499–500.

Nonstandard Units

You can measure length with different units.

You can use ⬭ as units.

You can use ⬚ as units.

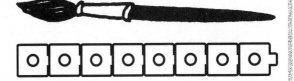

The paintbrush is **6** paper clips long.

The paintbrush is **8** cubes long.

Write the number of units.

1. About how many teaspoons long is your kitchen table?

My kitchen table is about _____ teaspoons long.

2. About how many toothpicks long is a pen?

A pen is about _____ toothpicks long.

3. About how many footsteps long is your bed?

My bed is about _____ footsteps long.

4. Measure your bed with a teaspoon. Why is the length different than the length measured with your feet?

Explain here.

Use with text pages 501–502.

Name _____ Date _____

Activity: Inches

You can estimate the length of an object in inches. Then you can measure the object with an inch ruler.

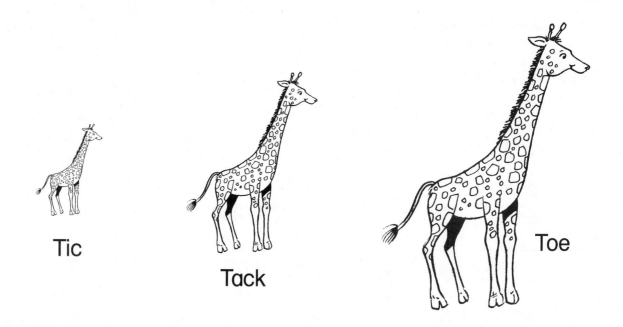

Tic

Tack

Toe

1. Use the picture. Complete the chart.

	Tic	Tack	Toe
Estimate	about _____ inches	about _____ inches	about _____ inches
Measure	about _____ inch	about _____ inches	about _____ inches

2. Estimate the length of a box of tissues. Measure the length.

Estimate: about _____ inches

Measure: about _____ inches

Use with text pages 503–505.

Name _____ Date _____

Centimeters

You can estimate the length of an object in centimeters.
Then you can measure the object with a centimeter ruler.

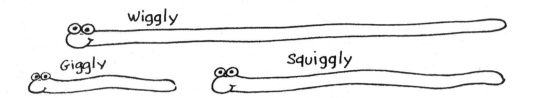

1. First estimate.
   Then use a centimeter ruler to measure.

	Giggly	Squiggly	Wiggly
Estimate	about _____ centimeters	about _____ centimeters	about _____ centimeters
Measure	about _____ centimeters	about _____ centimeters	about _____ centimeters

2. Find a small object in the kitchen.
   Estimate the length. Use a centimeter
   ruler to measure.

   Estimate: about _____ centimeters

   Measure: about _____ centimeters

Use with text pages 507–508.

Name _____ Date _____

Activity: Compare Weight

Objects may have different weights. A feather is lighter than a rock. A rock is heavier than a feather.

Find a tissue and a can of food. Circle the answer to the question.

1. Which feels heavier?

2. Which feels lighter?

Circle the heavier object.

3.

4.

Circle the lighter object.

5.

6.

7. Place three objects on a table. Order them from lightest to heaviest.

Write here.

1. _____

2. _____

3. _____

Use with text pages 511–512.

Name _____ Date _____

Activity: Pounds

You can measure weight in pounds.

A  weighs about 1 pound.

Circle the objects that weigh more than 1 pound.

1.

2.

Circle the objects that weigh less than 1 pound.

3.

4.

5. Look around your bedroom. Name an object less than 1 pound, an object about 1 pound, and an object more than 1 pound. Order the objects from lightest to heaviest.

Write here.

1. _____

2. _____

3. _____

Use with text pages 513–514.

Name _____ Date _____

Activity: Kilograms

You can measure how heavy an object is in kilograms.

A is about 1 kilogram.

Circle the object that is more than 1 kilogram.

1.

2.

Circle the object that is less than 1 kilogram.

3.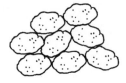

4.

5. Look around. Name an object less than 1 kilogram, an object about 1 kilogram, and an object more than 1 kilogram. Order the objects from lightest to heaviest.

Write here.

1. _____

2. _____

3. _____

Use with text pages 515–516.

Problem Solving:
Use Logical Reasoning

You can use clues to solve a problem.

Rick wants a new toy truck. It is smaller than the fire truck. It lifts dirt. Color the truck Rick wants.

Cross out the fire truck because Rick wants a smaller truck.
Cross out the van because it does not lift dirt.
Color the small truck that lifts dirt.

Solve. Color the object that matches the clues.

1. This truck has 4 wheels. It has a crane to pick up heavy boxes.

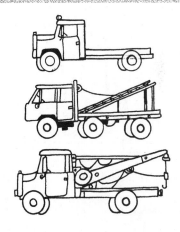

2. This truck is not the smallest truck. It has 8 wheels.

Use with text pages 517–518.

Name _____ Date _____

Activity: Compare and Order Capacity

Find the container that holds more.

Fill the teacup.

Pour the teacup into the glass.

The glass is not full, so it holds more than the cup.

Number the objects in order. **1** holds the least amount. **3** holds the greatest amount.

Try using real objects if you need help.

1.

_1_ _3_ _2_

2.

_____ _____ _____

3.

_____ _____ _____

4. Find containers with different shapes that hold about the same amount. Draw one pair.

Draw here.

Use with text pages 525–526.

Activity: Cups, Pints, and Quarts

You can use cups, pints, and quarts to tell how much a container holds.

2 cups = 1 pint   2 pints = 1 quart

Use a green crayon to color the ones that hold more.

1.

2.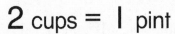

3.

4.

5. Find an empty quart container. Measure how many cups equal a quart.

Write or draw here.

Use with text pages 527–528.

Name _____ Date _____

Activity: Liters

You can use liters to tell how much a container holds.

less than **1** liter   **1** liter   more than **1** liter

Use a red crayon to color the objects that hold less than **1** liter.

1.

2.

Use a blue crayon to color the objects that hold more than **1** liter.

3.

4.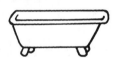

5. Find **3** containers. Use a **1** liter bottle to tell how much the containers can hold.

Write the results here.

_____

_____

_____

Use with text pages 529–531.

Name _____ Date _____

Temperature

You can use the words **hot** and **cold** to describe the temperature. Temperature is shown on a thermometer.

This thermometer shows the temperature is **95** degrees. That means it is very hot outside.

95 degrees

Draw a picture to show the temperature.

1. 20 degrees

2. 90 degrees

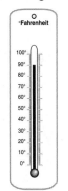

3. What is your favorite kind of weather? Work with a family member to draw the temperature in the thermometer and a picture to go with it.

°Fahrenheit

Draw here.

_____ degrees

Use with text pages 533–534.

Problem Solving: Reasonable Answers

Terry wants to line up her teddy bears from the shortest to the tallest. Circle the tool she should use to measure the height of the bears.

Circle the answer that makes more sense.

1. Sadie is making cookies. She needs sugar. What can she use to measure it?

2. Pedro has 2 rocks. He wants to know which is heavier. What can he use to find out?

3. Rita needs to know the temperature in her greenhouse. What can she use to find out?

4. Work with a family member to make up problems about what tools to use.

Draw or write here.

Use with text pages 535–536.

Name _____ Date _____

Doubles Plus One

Use a doubles to help you find other sums.

$7 + 7 =$ __14__

Add 1 more.

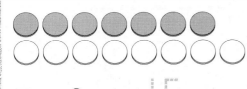
$7 + 8 =$ __15__

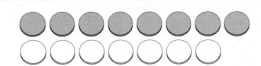
$8 + 7 =$ __15__

Find the sum.

1. $9 + 9 =$ ____

2. $10 + 9 =$ ____

3.
$$\begin{array}{r} 6 \\ + 6 \\ \hline \end{array}$$

4.
$$\begin{array}{r} 6 \\ + 7 \\ \hline \end{array}$$

5.
$$\begin{array}{r} 8 \\ + 8 \\ \hline \end{array}$$

6.
$$\begin{array}{r} 9 \\ + 8 \\ \hline \end{array}$$

7.
$$\begin{array}{r} 7 \\ + 7 \\ \hline \end{array}$$

8.
$$\begin{array}{r} 8 \\ + 7 \\ \hline \end{array}$$

9.
$$\begin{array}{r} 7 \\ + 8 \\ \hline \end{array}$$

10.
$$\begin{array}{r} 7 \\ + 6 \\ \hline \end{array}$$

11.
$$\begin{array}{r} 5 \\ + 5 \\ \hline \end{array}$$

12.
$$\begin{array}{r} 5 \\ + 6 \\ \hline \end{array}$$

13. Juan has 4 marbles. Mario
has 1 more marble than Juan.
How many marbles do they
have together?

Draw or write to explain.

Use with text pages 557–558.

Add with Ten

Use ten frames to add a number to 10.
Find $10 + 6$.

Show 10.

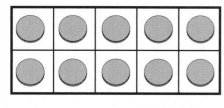

$10 + 6 = \underline{16}$

Show 6 more.

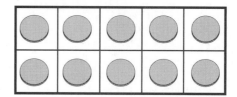

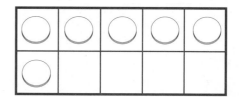

Find the sum.

1. $\begin{array}{r} 10 \\ + 5 \\ \hline \end{array}$
2. $\begin{array}{r} 10 \\ + 7 \\ \hline \end{array}$
3. $\begin{array}{r} 10 \\ + 3 \\ \hline \end{array}$
4. $\begin{array}{r} 2 \\ +10 \\ \hline \end{array}$
5. $\begin{array}{r} 8 \\ + 2 \\ \hline \end{array}$

6. $\begin{array}{r} 10 \\ + 6 \\ \hline \end{array}$
7. $\begin{array}{r} 10 \\ + 8 \\ \hline \end{array}$
8. $\begin{array}{r} 10 \\ + 2 \\ \hline \end{array}$
9. $\begin{array}{r} 10 \\ +10 \\ \hline \end{array}$
10. $\begin{array}{r} 3 \\ +10 \\ \hline \end{array}$

11. Sandi walks up 10 steps.
Then she walks up 4 more.
How many steps does she
walk up in all?

_____

Draw or write to explain.

Use with text pages 559–560.

Name _____ Date _____

Make a Ten to Add

Make a 10 to help you add 7, 8, or 9.
Find 7 + 4.

Show 7 + 4.

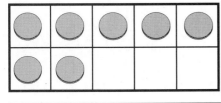

Make a 10.

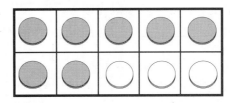
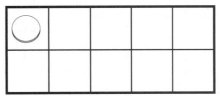

7 + 4 = _____

Add. Make a 10 first.

1. 8 + 4 = _____   2. 9 + 3 = _____

Add.

3. 9   4. 9   5. 9   6. 9   7. 9   8. 9
   + 5   + 4   + 3   + 6   + 8   + 9

9. 8   10. 8   11. 8   12. 8   13. 7   14. 7
   + 4   + 5   + 6   + 7   + 4   + 6

15. Ben has 8 books. He gets
    5 more books. How many
    books does he have now?

    _____ books

Draw or write to explain.

Use with text pages 561–562.

Addition Facts Practice

Find $6 + 7$.

Choose a way to add.

Order Property	Make a ten.	Use a doubles fact.
$6 + 7 = \underline{13}$	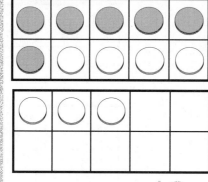	 
The order of addends can change. The sum is the same.	$6 + 7 = \underline{13}$	$6 + 6$ and 1 more.

Choose a way to add.
Find the sum.

1. $2 + 8 =$ _____

2. $6 + 5 =$ _____

3. $7 + 4 =$ _____

4. $7 + 7 =$ _____

5. $\begin{array}{r} 7 \\ + 8 \\ \hline \end{array}$
6. $\begin{array}{r} 9 \\ + 9 \\ \hline \end{array}$
7. $\begin{array}{r} 8 \\ + 9 \\ \hline \end{array}$
8. $\begin{array}{r} 5 \\ + 7 \\ \hline \end{array}$
9. $\begin{array}{r} 4 \\ + 8 \\ \hline \end{array}$

Choose a way to add.
Find the sum.

10. $4 + 4 =$ _____

11. $5 + 6 =$ _____

12. $6 + 6 =$ _____

13. $9 + 8 =$ _____

14. $8 + 9 =$ _____

15. $6 + 8 =$ _____

Use with text pages 565–568.

Names for Numbers

Use different ways to make the same sum.

Names for 16

Whole	
16	
Part	Part
9	7

Whole	
16	
Part	Part
8	8

Find different names for the number.

1.

Whole	
12	
Part	Part

Whole	
12	
Part	Part

Whole	
12	
Part	Part

Whole	
12	
Part	Part

2.

Whole	
15	
Part	Part

Whole	
15	
Part	Part

3.

Whole	
14	
Part	Part

Whole	
14	
Part	Part

Find the missing part.

4.

Whole	
11	
Part	Part
	8

5.

Whole	
13	
Part	Part
6	

6.

Whole	
18	
Part	Part
	9

Use with text pages 569–570.

Add Three Numbers

Look for facts you know to help you add three numbers.

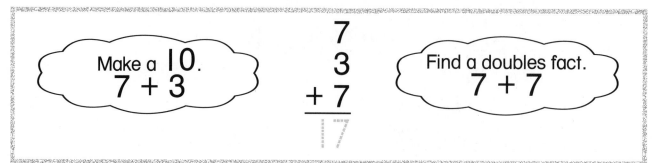

Make a 10.
7 + 3

7
3
+ 7
———
17

Find a doubles fact.
7 + 7

Add.

1.   5
     2
   + 5
   ———

2.   8
     2
   + 6
   ———

3.   6
     6
   + 3
   ———

4.   1
     9
   + 7
   ———

5.   9
     7
   + 2
   ———

6. 6 + 4 + 3 = _____   7. 4 + 3 + 7 = _____

8. 2 + 9 + 2 = _____   9. 3 + 1 + 7 = _____

Solve.

10. Lisa scored 3 points in Game 3.

    How many points did she score in all?

Lisa	Points
Game 1	5
Game 2	5
Game 3	

_____ + _____ + _____ = _____

Use with text pages 571–572.

Write a Number Sentence

The Red team and the Blue team play tag.
Each team has 8 players.
How many players are there altogether?

_____ players on the Red team.

_____ players on the Blue team.

Solve. Write a number sentence.

$8 + 8 = 16$ _____ players

16

Write a number sentence to solve.

1. Lou scores 5 points. Ivan scores 9 points. How many points do they score in all?

   ____ ◯ ____ ◯ ____

   _____ points

---

2. The T-ball team has 8 boys and 7 girls. How many players are on the team altogether?

   ____ ◯ ____ ◯ ____

   _____ players

---

3. Erin's team brings 8 oranges to practice. Ali's team brings 6. How many oranges do the teams have in all?

   ____ ◯ ____ ◯ ____

   _____ oranges

Use with text pages 573–575.

Use Doubles to Subtract

Find $16 - 8$.

Use a doubles fact to help you subtract.

$8 + 8 =$ ___16___

So, $16 - 8 =$ ___8___

Add. Then subtract.

1. $5 + 5 =$ _____

   $10 - 5 =$ _____

2. $6 + 6 =$ _____

   $12 - 6 =$ _____

---

3. $10 + 10 =$ _____

   $20 - 10 =$ _____

4. $9 + 9 =$ _____

   $18 - 9 =$ _____

---

5. $\begin{array}{r} 3 \\ +3 \\ \hline \end{array}$ $\begin{array}{r} 6 \\ -3 \\ \hline \end{array}$

6. $\begin{array}{r} 4 \\ +4 \\ \hline \end{array}$ $\begin{array}{r} 8 \\ -4 \\ \hline \end{array}$

7. $\begin{array}{r} 8 \\ +8 \\ \hline \end{array}$ $\begin{array}{r} 16 \\ -\ 8 \\ \hline \end{array}$

8. $\begin{array}{r} 7 \\ +7 \\ \hline \end{array}$ $\begin{array}{r} 14 \\ -\ 7 \\ \hline \end{array}$

Solve.

Draw or write to explain.

9. Tom is 5 years old. In how many years will he be 10?

_____ years

Use with text pages 583–584.

Parts and Wholes

If you know the whole and one of the parts, you can find the other part.

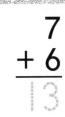

$$7 + 6$$

Workmat 3

Whole	
13	
Part	**Part**
7	?

$$13 - 7$$ $$13 - 6$$

Think
7 and what other
part make 13?

Write the difference.

1. $$13 - 9$$ $$13 - 4$$

2. $$14 - 6$$ $$14 - 8$$

3. $$12 - 8$$ $$12 - 4$$

4. $$13 - 5$$ $$13 - 8$$

5. $$14 - 5$$ $$14 - 9$$

6. $$12 - 5$$ $$12 - 7$$

Use the numbers to write an addition fact.

Then write the related subtraction facts.

$$5 + 8 \over 13$$

7. _____ + _____ = _____

8. _____ − _____ = _____

9. _____ − _____ = _____

Use with text pages 585–586.

Relate Addition and Subtraction Facts

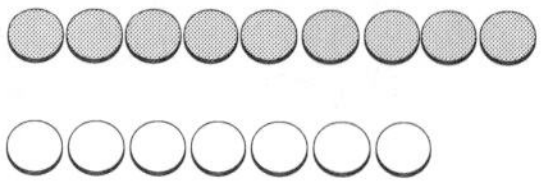

$$9 + 7$$ ●●●●●●●●●
○○○○○○○
16
$$16 - 9$$
$$16 - 7$$

Add.

Then find the difference.

1. $$7 + 8$$ $$15 - 7$$ $$15 - 8$$

2. $$10 + 5$$ $$15 - 10$$ $$15 - 5$$

3. $$6 + 9$$ $$15 - 6$$ $$15 - 9$$

4. $$10 + 6$$ $$16 - 10$$ $$16 - 6$$

5. $$9 + 5$$ $$14 - 9$$ $$14 - 5$$

6. $$8 + 5$$ $$13 - 8$$ $$13 - 5$$

Solve.

7. Sixteen minus seven equals _____.

8. Fifteen minus five equals _____.

Use with text pages 587–588.

Subtract From 17 through 20

Use an addition fact to help you subtract.

```
  1 0
+   9
-----
  1 9
```

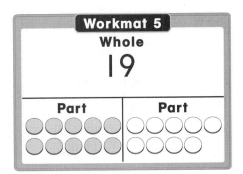

Workmat 5
Whole
1 9

| Part | Part |

```
  1 9        1 9
- 1 0       -   9
-----       -----
    9         1 0
```

Subtract.

1.
```
  1 7
-   9
-----
```

2.
```
  2 0
- 1 0
-----
```

3.
```
  1 9
-   9
-----
```

4.
```
  1 6
-   8
-----
```

5.
```
  1 5
- 1 0
-----
```

6.
```
  1 8
-   8
-----
```

7.
```
  1 7
-   7
-----
```

8.
```
  1 6
-   9
-----
```

9.
```
  1 9
- 1 0
-----
```

10.
```
  1 8
- 1 0
-----
```

11.
```
  1 6
-   7
-----
```

12.
```
  1 5
-   6
-----
```

13.
```
  1 7
- 1 0
-----
```

14.
```
  1 8
-   9
-----
```

15.
```
  1 5
-   8
-----
```

16.
```
  1 6
- 1 0
-----
```

17.
```
  1 4
-   9
-----
```

18.
```
  1 2
-   8
-----
```

Write the missing number.

19. $20 - \underline{\quad} = 10$

20. $17 - \underline{\quad} = 9$

21. $19 - \underline{\quad} = 9$

22. $18 - \underline{\quad} = 0$

Use with text pages 591–592.

Subtraction Facts Practice

You can use different strategies to find differences.

Use doubles. $14 - 7 = 7$ $7 + 7 = 14$

Use parts and wholes.

Whole
17

Part	Part
9	?

$17 - 9 = 8$

$17 - 8 = 9$

Relate addition and subtraction. $8 + 7 = 15$ $15 - 7 = 8$

Find the difference.

1. $13 - 4 =$ _____

2. $16 - 7 =$ _____

3. $15 - 8 =$ _____

4. $18 - 9 =$ _____

5. $16 - 9 =$ _____

6. $14 - 6 =$ _____

7.
$$\begin{array}{r} 19 \\ -\ 7 \\ \hline \end{array}$$

8.
$$\begin{array}{r} 17 \\ -\ 8 \\ \hline \end{array}$$

9.
$$\begin{array}{r} 20 \\ -\ 10 \\ \hline \end{array}$$

Solve.

10. Lin needs to find $13 - 8$. What addition fact can help him?

Draw or write to explain.

_____ + _____ = 13

Use with text pages 593–596.

Name _____ Date _____

Fact Families

The 4 related facts make a fact family.

16	
9	7

$$9 + 7 = \underline{16}$$

$$7 + 9 = \underline{16}$$

$$16 - 9 = \underline{7}$$

$$16 - 7 = \underline{9}$$

Complete the fact family.

1.

13	
8	5

$$8 + 5 = \underline{}$$

$$\underline{} + \underline{} = \underline{}$$

$$13 - 5 = \underline{}$$

$$\underline{} - \underline{} = \underline{}$$

2.

15	
9	6

$$9 + 6 = \underline{}$$

$$\underline{} + \underline{} = \underline{}$$

$$15 - 9 = \underline{}$$

$$\underline{} - \underline{} = \underline{}$$

3. Color the △ green.
Color the ○ red.

Write a fact family to tell about the shapes.

____ + ____ = ____ | ____ − ____ = ____

____ + ____ = ____ | ____ − ____ = ____

Use with text pages 597–598.

Problem Solving:
Too Much Information

Choose the information that you need.
Cross out information that you do not need.

José finds 18 sand dollars.
~~Then he finds 3 starfish.~~
Later he finds 9 clam shells.
How many more sand dollars than
clam shells did José find?

__18__ – __9__ = __9__

__9__ more sand dollars

Cross out the information you do not need.
Solve.   Draw or write to explain.

1. There are 15 boats in the
   harbor. It is 7 o'clock in the
   morning. Now 6 boats sail
   away. How many boats are
   still in the harbor?

2. Zoe's class has 2 teachers.
   The class of 17 children play
   on the beach. 9 children
   go for snacks. How many
   children are still playing?

Use with text pages 599–600.

Mental Math: Add Tens

An addition fact can help you add tens.

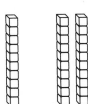

$1 + 2 = \underline{3}$

1 ten $+ 2$ tens $= \underline{3}$ tens

$\underline{10} + \underline{20} = \underline{30}$

Complete the addition sentences.

1.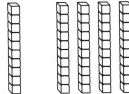

$1 + 4 = \underline{\quad}$

1 ten $+ 4$ tens $= \underline{\quad}$ tens

$\underline{\quad} + \underline{\quad} = \underline{\quad}$

2.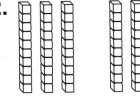

$3 + 2 = \underline{\quad}$

3 tens $+ 2$ tens $= \underline{\quad}$ tens

$\underline{\quad} + \underline{\quad} = \underline{\quad}$

3. 2 tens $+ 7$ tens $= \underline{\quad}$ tens

$\underline{\quad} + \underline{\quad} = \underline{\quad}$

4. 6 tens $+ 3$ tens $= \underline{\quad}$ tens

$\underline{\quad} + \underline{\quad} = \underline{\quad}$

5. Jack puts 40 marbles in a box. Then he puts in more. Now there are 70 marbles in the box. How many more marbles did he put in?

_____ marbles

Draw or write to explain.

Use with text pages 607–608.

Add With Two-Digit Numbers

Find $52 + 6$.

Add the ones.

Tens	Ones
5	2
+	6
	8

Think
$2 + 6 = 8$

Add the tens.

Tens	Ones
5	2
+	6
5	8

So, $52 + 6 = 58$.

Add. Write the sum.

1.

Tens	Ones
3	4
+	2

2.

Tens	Ones
4	1
+	5

3.

Tens	Ones
6	3
+	4

4.

Tens	Ones
2	5
+	3

5.

Tens	Ones
8	7
+	2

6.

Tens	Ones
7	6
+	1

7.

Tens	Ones
9	4
+	3

8.

Tens	Ones
5	5
+	4

9.

Tens	Ones
9	0
+	5

10.

Tens	Ones
6	4
+	2

11.

Tens	Ones
3	1
+	8

Use with text pages 609–610.

Add Two-Digit Numbers

Find 43 + 25.

Think
Add the ones. Then add
4 tens + 2 tens.

Tens	Ones
4	3
+ 2	5
6	8

Add. Write the sum.

1.
Tens	Ones
2	2
+ 1	4

2.
Tens	Ones
5	6
+ 3	2

3.
Tens	Ones
3	8
+ 2	0

4.
Tens	Ones
7	5
+ 2	3

5.
Tens	Ones
1	7
+ 4	2

6.
Tens	Ones
6	3
+ 2	3

7.
Tens	Ones
5	0
+ 2	9

8.
Tens	Ones
3	3
+ 5	4

9.
Tens	Ones
6	1
+ 2	4

10.
Tens	Ones
4	5
+ 3	0

11.
Tens	Ones
8	4
+ 1	3

12.
Tens	Ones
6	5
+ 2	4

13. Sara has 25 baseball cards. Joe has 10 baseball cards. How many baseball cards do they have in all?

_____ baseball cards

Draw or write to explain.

Use with text pages 611–612.

Name _____ Date _____

Different Ways to Add

Use mental math.

Tens	Ones
3	0
+ 2	0
5	0

Use paper and pencil.

Tens	Ones
4	7
+ 1	2
5	9

Choose a way to add. Write the sum.

1.
Tens	Ones
4	5
+	1

2.
Tens	Ones
5	3
+ 2	5

3.
Tens	Ones
1	6
+ 2	3

4. 20
   + 3

5. 44
  + 11

6. 62
  + 10

7. 24
  + 34

8. 60
  + 5

9. 33
  + 20

10. 21
   + 48

11. 76
   + 10

12. 30 + 10 = _____

13. 55 + 1 = _____

14. Ray picks 13 red apples. Then he picks 12 yellow apples. How many apples does he pick?

Draw or write to explain.

_____ apples

Use with text pages 615–616.

Two-Digit Addition Practice

Remember to add the ones first, then add the tens.

Add. Color each box to match the sum.

Sums 20 to 49	Sums 50 to 79
Red	Blue

1. $\begin{array}{r} 70 \\ +\ 7 \\ \hline \end{array}$

2. $\begin{array}{r} 33 \\ +\ 5 \\ \hline \end{array}$

3. $\begin{array}{r} 15 \\ +13 \\ \hline \end{array}$

4. $\begin{array}{r} 53 \\ +23 \\ \hline \end{array}$

5. $\begin{array}{r} 10 \\ +30 \\ \hline \end{array}$

6. $\begin{array}{r} 17 \\ +41 \\ \hline \end{array}$

7. $\begin{array}{r} 11 \\ +61 \\ \hline \end{array}$

8. $\begin{array}{r} 60 \\ +\ 3 \\ \hline \end{array}$

9. Stan makes 21 cards. His sister makes 14 cards. How many cards do they make?

Draw or write to explain.

_____ + _____ = _____ cards

Use with text pages 617–618.

Guess and Check

Jeremy needs 19 bagels for a party.
Which 2 boxes does Jeremy buy?

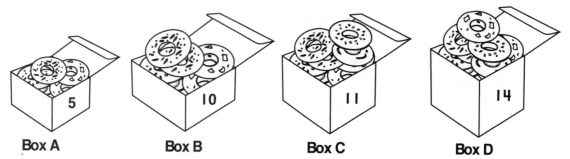

Box A   Box B   Box C   Box D

Make a guess. Add to check the guess.

First Guess

Box A   5
Box B   + 10
          ‾‾‾‾
            15

Too few.

Second Guess

Box A   5
Box D   + 14
          ‾‾‾‾
            19

*This is
the answer.*

Jeremy needs Box A and Box D.

Use Guess and Check to solve.

1. Saul gets bagels for his
   swim team. He needs
   25 bagels. Which two
   boxes does he buy?

   Draw or write to explain.

   Box _____ and Box _____

2. Mrs. Sanchez brings food
   for the class. She needs
   21 bagels. Which
   2 boxes does she buy?

   Box _____ and Box _____

Use with text pages 619–621.

Mental Math: Subtract Tens

A subtraction fact can help you subtract tens.

$8 - 5 =$ __3__

8 tens $- 5$ tens $=$ __3__ tens

__80__ $-$ __50__ $=$ __30__

Complete the subtraction sentences.

1. $6 - 1 =$ ____

   6 tens $- 1$ ten $=$ ____ tens

   ____ $-$ ____ $=$ ____

2. $4 - 3 =$ ____

   4 tens $- 3$ tens $=$ ____ ten

   ____ $-$ ____ $=$ ____

3. 9 tens $- 6$ tens $=$ ____ tens

   ____ $-$ ____ $=$ ____

4. 7 tens $- 3$ tens $=$ ____ tens

   ____ $-$ ____ $=$ ____

5. 5 tens $- 2$ tens $=$ ____ tens

   ____ $-$ ____ $=$ ____

6. 8 tens $- 4$ tens $=$ ____ tens

   ____ $-$ ____ $=$ ____

7. The art class has 30 children.
   The music class has 20 children.
   How many more children are in
   the art class?

Draw or write to explain.

_____ more children

Use with text pages 629–630.

Name _____ Date _____

Subtract With Two-Digit Numbers

Find 37 − 6.

Subtract the ones.

Tens	Ones
3	7
−	6

Subtract the tens.

Tens	Ones
3	7
−	6
3	1

Subtract. Write the difference.

1.

Tens	Ones
2	7
−	2

2.

Tens	Ones
2	5
−	3

3.

Tens	Ones
3	9
−	8

4.

Tens	Ones
2	6
−	6

5.

Tens	Ones
5	7
−	6

6.

Tens	Ones
4	6
−	3

7.

Tens	Ones
6	8
−	4

8.

Tens	Ones
5	4
−	2

9. Paula has 79¢. She gives her brother 6¢. How much does Paula have left?

_____ ¢

Draw or write to explain.

Use with text pages 631–632.

Subtract Two-Digit Numbers

Find 48 − 25.

Tens	Ones
4	8
− 2	5
2	3

Remember
First subtract the ones.
Then subtract the tens.

Subtract. Write the difference.

1.

Tens	Ones
2	9
− 1	4
1	5

2.

Tens	Ones
3	6
− 2	1

3.

Tens	Ones
4	1
− 2	0

4.

Tens	Ones
4	8
− 1	6

5.

Tens	Ones
5	9
− 3	8

6.

Tens	Ones
5	7
− 3	7

7.

Tens	Ones
6	8
− 2	4

8.

Tens	Ones
7	7
− 3	6

9.

Tens	Ones
8	4
− 1	1

10.

Tens	Ones
9	5
− 6	2

11.

Tens	Ones
8	9
− 2	2

12.

Tens	Ones
9	9
− 4	5

13. Mr. Jones cooks 18 pancakes for breakfast. He gives 10 pancakes to his family. How many pancakes are left?

Draw or write to explain.

_____ pancakes

Use with text pages 633–634.

Different Ways to Subtract

Use mental math.

Tens	Ones
7	0
− 2	0
5	0

Use paper and pencil.

Tens	Ones
6	4
− 4	3
2	1

Choose a way to subtract.
Write the difference.

1.
Tens	Ones
3	8
−	2

2.
Tens	Ones
8	7
− 3	5

3.
Tens	Ones
5	9
− 4	7

4.
Tens	Ones
7	3
− 5	2

5.
```
   45
 −  3
```

6.
```
   76
 − 24
```

7.
```
   40
 − 20
```

8.
```
   89
 − 55
```

9.
```
   94
 − 21
```

10.
```
   37
 − 10
```

11.
```
   68
 −  8
```

12.
```
   53
 − 23
```

13. $90 - 30 =$ _____

14. $84 - 2 =$ _____

15. Paul has 40 marbles. He gives 10 marbles to his sister. How many marbles does Paul have now?

_____ marbles

Draw or write to explain.

Use with text pages 635–636.

Two-Digit Subtraction Practice

Find $69 - 34$.

Subtract the ones.

$$\begin{array}{r} 69 \\ -\ 34 \\ \hline 5 \end{array}$$

Subtract the tens.

$$\begin{array}{r} 69 \\ -\ 34 \\ \hline 35 \end{array}$$

Subtract.

1. $\begin{array}{r} 88 \\ -\ 24 \\ \hline 64 \end{array}$

2. $\begin{array}{r} 47 \\ -\ 17 \\ \hline \end{array}$

3. $\begin{array}{r} 80 \\ -\ 50 \\ \hline \end{array}$

4. $\begin{array}{r} 39 \\ -\ 11 \\ \hline \end{array}$

5. $\begin{array}{r} 75 \\ -\ \ 4 \\ \hline \end{array}$

6. $\begin{array}{r} 56 \\ -\ 45 \\ \hline \end{array}$

7. $\begin{array}{r} 31 \\ -\ 10 \\ \hline \end{array}$

8. $\begin{array}{r} 94 \\ -\ 62 \\ \hline \end{array}$

9. $\begin{array}{r} 98 \\ -\ 20 \\ \hline \end{array}$

10. $\begin{array}{r} 39 \\ -\ \ 6 \\ \hline \end{array}$

11. $\begin{array}{r} 65 \\ -\ 23 \\ \hline \end{array}$

12. $\begin{array}{r} 82 \\ -\ \ 2 \\ \hline \end{array}$

13. Marco has 32 baseball cards. He gives 12 cards to Ken. How many cards does Marco have left?

Draw or write to explain.

_____ cards

Use with text pages 639–640.

Check Subtraction

Add to check subtraction.

$$\begin{array}{r} 67 \\ -41 \\ \hline 26 \end{array} \qquad \begin{array}{r} 26 \\ +41 \\ \hline 67 \end{array}$$

If the sum equals the number you subtracted from, your answer is correct.

Subtract. Check by adding.

1.
$$\begin{array}{r} 59 \\ -42 \\ \hline \end{array}$$
$+$ ☐ ☐ / ☐

2.
$$\begin{array}{r} 80 \\ -20 \\ \hline \end{array}$$
$+$ ☐ ☐ / ☐

3.
$$\begin{array}{r} 48 \\ -23 \\ \hline \end{array}$$
$+$ ☐ ☐ / ☐

4.
$$\begin{array}{r} 96 \\ -55 \\ \hline \end{array}$$
$+$ ☐ ☐ / ☐

5.
$$\begin{array}{r} 37 \\ -3 \\ \hline \end{array}$$
$+$ ☐ ☐ / ☐

6.
$$\begin{array}{r} 75 \\ -21 \\ \hline \end{array}$$
$+$ ☐ ☐ / ☐

7. Maria subtracts $65 - 22$ and gets the answer 43. Show how she can add to check her subtraction.

Draw or write to explain.

Use with text pages 641–642.

Choose the Operation

You can use addition or subtraction
to help you solve problems.

The Kwan family likes macaroni.
They have 11 boxes of long macaroni.
They have 8 boxes of short macaroni.
How many boxes do they have?

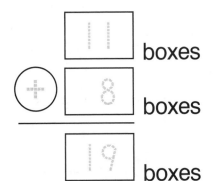

boxes

boxes

boxes

Add to solve.

_____ boxes of macaroni

---

1. The King family has 15 cans
of soup. They have 7 cans of
chicken soup. The rest are
tomato soup. How many cans
of tomato soup do they have?

cans

cans

cans

_____ cans of tomato soup

---

2. Brendan counts 48 fish in
the water. Then 17 fish
swim away. How many
fish are left?

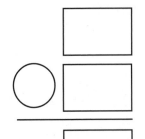

_____ fish

Use with text pages 643–645.